Praise for

A LAYMAN'S GUIDE TO ARTIFICIAL INTELLIGENCE

Having gone through the contents of "*A Layman's Guide to Artificial Intelligence*," I absolutely loved the way it has been structured. The book masterfully tells the story of AI, from its origins to where it stands today, making it both engaging and informative. It covers almost everything a layperson or even a professional would want to know to get started with AI. The storytelling approach makes complex topics easy to grasp, keeping the reader hooked throughout. Finally, the section about the authors Kalyanjit and Pratibha, is truly impressive, highlighting their expertise and passion for making AI accessible to all. Very warm congratulations to them and wishing this book a huge success!

Manash Deka
Senior Cloud Architect/ Technology Lead, HCLTech

~~~~*******~~~~

"*A Layman's Guide to Artificial Intelligence*" is a super approachable and informative read for anyone curious about AI. The authors do a great job of breaking down complicated tech stuff into simple, everyday language that's easy to follow. I really liked how they included real-life examples—from health care to self-driving cars—
~~~~

that show how AI is already part of our lives. It's not just about the tech though—they also talk about the big-picture stuff like ethics and the future of AI, which keeps it interesting. The tone is friendly and not too heavy, so it never feels overwhelming. If you're new to AI or just want a clearer idea of what it's all about, this book is a great place to start.

Arshad Perwez
Macro Strategist, SBI Mutual Fund

~~~~*******~~~~

A Clear and Accessible Introduction to AI: This book is a good starting point for anyone curious about Artificial Intelligence. It provides a broad overview of key concepts, explains what falls under the umbrella of AI, and introduces new terms in a way that's easy to grasp—even if you have no technical background.

What I appreciated most was how the author kept the language simple and beginner-friendly. It really feels like the book was written with the reader in mind, making complex ideas more digestible.

Despite that, it's a solid resource and serves its purpose well. If you're just getting into AI and want a no-pressure introduction, this book is a worthwhile pick.

Natasha Mahesh
AI Enthusiast

~~~~*******~~~~

As a technologist, I approached Arc with a healthy mix of curiosity and scepticism—wondering whether a "*layman's guide*" could offer any real depth. To my surprise, the book manages to strike a thoughtful balance: it simplifies without dumbing down, and contextualises AI's impact in a way that even seasoned professionals can appreciate.

The healthcare section, in particular, reflects a clear understanding of how AI is being applied in the real world. It covers key use cases—diagnostics, personalised medicine, drug discovery, and administrative automation—with clarity and relevance. The discussion on AI-powered diagnostics, such as systems that analyse X-rays or predict chronic conditions, aligns with what we're actively developing and deploying in the healthtech space.

I also appreciated the book's emphasis on ethical considerations—bias in training data, transparency in decision-making, and safety in clinical environments. These aren't just theoretical concerns; they are daily design and governance challenges we face when building and scaling AI systems in regulated industries.

While Arc isn't meant for a technical deep dive, it's an effective primer for stakeholders across disciplines—clinicians, product managers, policy leaders—who need to understand the "why" behind AI adoption. For technologists, it's a useful framing tool to align with non-technical teams and drive more informed conversations.

Bottom line: Arc is a smart, concise, and responsible introduction to AI. It won't teach you how to build models—but it will remind you why building them thoughtfully matters.

Shashank Garg
Founder & CEO, The Zen India

~~~~*******~~~~

"*A Layman's Guide to Artificial Intelligence*" by Pratibha and Kalyanjit Hatibaruah is an excellent starting point for anyone curious about AI. As a software testing professional, I found the book clear, informative, and beginner-friendly. It explains complex concepts like machine learning, deep learning, and NLP in simple terms. The real-world examples and ethical discussions add great context. The book balances technical insights with practical applications across industries. Whether you're from IT or not, this guide builds a solid foundation in AI without overwhelming you. Highly recommended for anyone stepping into the world of artificial intelligence.

Munish Paikara
IT Professional

~~~~*******~~~~

A Layman's Guide
Artificial Intelligence

By

Pratibha Das Hatibaruah
& Kalyanjit Hatibaruah

This book aims to provide a foundational understanding of Artificial Intelligence in a simple and engaging way. While every effort has been made to ensure accuracy, readers should consider this book as a general guide to exploring AI and not a substitute for professional technical, ethical, or legal advice.

Although the authors and publisher have made every effort to ensure that the information in this book is accurate at the time of publication, they assume no responsibility for errors, inaccuracies, omissions, or inconsistencies. They disclaim any liability for any loss, damage, or disruption caused by errors or omissions, whether resulting from negligence, accident, or any other cause.

This book may include references to third-party sources, technologies, and platforms; their inclusion does not imply endorsement or affiliation.

ISBN: 978-93-342-1977-7

Published by Flugel Publishing House

Dedication

♣ To Every Reader Who Seeks to Understand ♣

To every reader who finds a part of themselves here —

May this book be a mirror to your curiosity,
a map through the maze of modern machines,
or simply a moment of pause to marvel at possibility.

In a world shaped by algorithms and logic,
may you always discover the human spark –
in understanding, in questioning, in wonder.

Contents

Preface

Artificial Intelligence, or AI, is no longer a thing of the future—it's already here, quietly working behind the scenes in our daily lives. Whether you're using Siri to set a reminder, asking Alexa to play your favourite song, or wondering how Netflix always seems to know what you want to watch next—AI is at play.

You don't need to be a tech expert to notice that AI is changing the world. But for many people, the words "artificial intelligence" still feel confusing or even a bit scary. It can seem too technical, too fast-moving, or just not something for "ordinary" people to understand. We wrote this book to prove that this isn't true.

This book is for anyone who's curious about AI—how it works, where we see it in everyday life, and what it means for our future. If you've ever asked questions like *"How does my phone understand what I'm saying?"* or *"Can AI make decisions on its own?"* or *"Will robots take all our jobs?"*, then you're in the right place.

Based on our experience of teaching and running workshops, we've written this guide in a clear, friendly way that avoids complex jargon. We use simple language and real-life examples to explain the basics first, then gently guide you towards deeper ideas like machine learning, neural networks, and natural language processing (NLP). We revisit important ideas throughout the book, and you may notice some concepts are repeated—that's to help make things clearer as we go and to help you reconnect the dots if things feel tricky at times, especially given the complexity of the technology.

This book won't turn you into an AI engineer, and it doesn't need to. It's here to help you feel confident and informed, to understand what AI really is (and isn't), and to see how it touches your life in ways you might not have noticed before.

We hope ***A Layman's Guide to Artificial Intelligence*** helps you feel ready to be part of the conversation around one of the most important technologies of our time.

Pratibha Das Hatibaruah
Kalyanjit Hatibaruah

Chapter 1
Unleashing the Power of Artificial Intelligence

What is AI?

Artificial Intelligence (AI) is transforming the world around us. Whether it's the voice assistants we use on our phones or the tailored recommendations we get from streaming services, AI is all around us. But what does AI truly mean, and why is it so crucial now?

At its core, AI refers to machines and computers that can perform tasks that typically require human intelligence. These tasks include things like learning from experience, making decisions, solving problems, and understanding language. Essentially, AI allows machines to "think" and "learn," which makes them more adaptable, efficient, and capable of handling complex tasks.

This technology is not just about automating work—it's about revolutionising how we live, work, and interact with the world. AI is already being used in countless industries, from healthcare and education to entertainment and transportation, and its potential is only growing.

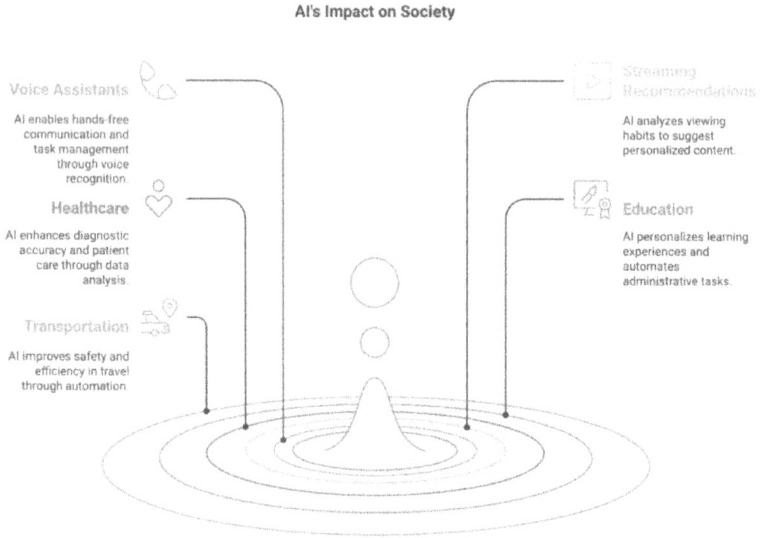

Understanding AI

AI might sound like something from a science fiction movie, but in reality, it's a rapidly evolving field of technology. When we talk about AI, we are actually referring to different types of systems and technologies. For example, machine learning is a subset of AI that focuses on teaching computers to learn from data and experience, much like humans do. The more data the system receives, the better it gets at making predictions and decisions.

There's also natural language processing (NLP), which helps machines understand and interpret human language. This allows systems like Siri, Alexa, and Google Assistant to understand your voice commands and respond in a way that feels natural.

Computer vision is another area of AI that allows machines to see and interpret the world around them, just like humans do. For instance, facial recognition technology used in security systems relies on AI to recognise and identify faces from images or video feeds.

AI in Simple Terms

In simple terms, AI is about making computers smarter by teaching them how to solve problems on their own. Just as humans learn from experience and use that knowledge to make better decisions, AI systems are trained to process large amounts of information, identify patterns, and use this knowledge to improve their performance.

Picture yourself explaining the rules of a game to a young child. At first, they might not know the rules, but as they play more and experience different situations, they learn and get better at it. AI works similarly. It starts with basic knowledge and becomes more skilled as it encounters more data and experiences.

Narrow AI vs. General AI

When we talk about AI, it's important to understand that there are two main types: **Narrow AI** and **General AI**.

- **Narrow AI** (also called Weak AI) is the type of AI we interact with most frequently. It's designed to do a specific task, like recommending movies on Netflix, detecting fraudulent transactions in your bank account, or helping you navigate with GPS. Narrow AI is great at what it does, but it's limited to that one task.

- **General AI** (or Strong AI) is the kind of AI you might see in science fiction films, like robots that can think, learn, and reason in the same way humans do. Unlike Narrow AI, General AI would be capable of performing any intellectual task that a human can, from cooking dinner to solving world problems. While General AI is still a concept and hasn't been fully realised yet, it's an area of active research and may become a reality in the future.

How Does AI Work?

AI works through algorithms, which are simply sets of instructions or rules that tell the computer how to perform a task. These algorithms are trained using data, which helps the system "learn" and improve over time. For example, an AI system designed to recognise pictures of dogs and cats would be trained with thousands of images, and over time, it would become better at distinguishing between the two.

This process is known as machine learning, and it's what enables AI to perform tasks without being explicitly programmed for every situation. The more data the AI system gets, the smarter it becomes.

One example of machine learning is supervised learning, where the AI system is given data with known answers (like a set of pictures labelled as "dog" or "cat"). The AI processes this data to recognise patterns and generate predictions. Eventually, it can apply what it has learned to new, unseen data.

The Role of AI in Our Lives

AI is not just a tool for tech experts—it's something that's becoming part of daily life for most people. We may not always realise it, but AI is helping us in many areas, often making our lives easier without us even thinking about it.

In Healthcare: AI helps doctors diagnose diseases more accurately by analysing medical data, images, and patient records. For example, AI systems can spot early signs of diseases like cancer by analysing X-rays or MRIs with incredible precision. AI is also being used to develop personalised treatment plans, which means doctors can tailor care to individual patients.

In Transportation: AI is behind the development of autonomous vehicles (self-driving cars). These cars use AI to understand their surroundings, make decisions, and navigate safely without human intervention. While fully autonomous cars are still in development, AI is already making our roads safer by helping drivers with navigation, accident avoidance, and traffic prediction.

In Finance: AI is helping banks and financial institutions detect fraud and optimise trading strategies. By analysing patterns in transactions, AI can identify suspicious activities and alert security teams to take action. AI is also being used in personal finance apps to help users make better decisions about their spending and saving.

In Entertainment: If you've ever used Netflix or YouTube, you've encountered AI in action. These platforms use AI to recommend movies and videos based on your preferences, helping you discover new content you might enjoy. The more you watch, the smarter the recommendations become, making it feel like the system "knows" you.

Ethical Considerations of AI

While AI offers numerous benefits, it also brings up important ethical questions. For instance, AI systems are trained using data, and if that data is biased or flawed, the AI system can make unfair decisions. This is a big concern in areas like hiring, law enforcement, and healthcare.

For example, if an AI system is trained on historical data where a certain group of people has been unfairly treated, the system may unknowingly perpetuate that bias. This is why it's crucial to ensure that AI systems are fair, transparent, and accountable.

There's also the issue of privacy. AI systems often rely on collecting vast amounts of personal data to function, and it's important to ensure that this data is used responsibly. People must be informed about how their data is being used and have control over it.

The Future of AI

The future of AI is incredibly exciting, but it's also full of challenges. As AI continues to evolve, it's expected to play a larger role in many aspects of our lives. In the future, AI could help solve some of the world's biggest problems, like climate change, poverty, and healthcare access.

AI might be used to predict environmental changes and suggest ways to reduce carbon footprints. It could also assist in scientific research by quickly analysing vast amounts of data to find solutions to complex problems.

However, as AI becomes more powerful, we must ensure that it's developed and used in a way that benefits everyone. This includes creating regulations to ensure AI is used ethically and responsibly, as well as making sure it doesn't replace human workers but rather complements their skills.

Conclusion: Embracing AI for a Better Future

AI is here, and it's reshaping the world. While we're still just scratching the surface of what AI can do, its potential is immense. From improving healthcare to revolutionising transportation, AI promises to make our lives easier, more efficient, and more connected.

But with great power comes great responsibility. As we move forward, it's essential to develop AI in a way that is ethical, transparent, and fair. By doing so, we can ensure that AI is a force for good, benefiting society and improving the quality of life for everyone.

Embracing AI doesn't just mean adopting new technologies—it means shaping a future where humans and machines work together to solve problems, create new opportunities, and build a better world for generations to come.

Chapter 2
Goals of AI Research

The field of artificial intelligence (AI) is driven by a range of research objectives aimed at pushing the boundaries of technology and applying it to real-world problems. These goals span across various domains, encompassing technical, ethical, and societal dimensions. Understanding the aims of AI research helps shed light on its direction and potential impact on society.

1. Development of General Intelligence (AGI)

A central objective in AI research is the pursuit of Artificial General Intelligence (AGI). AGI refers to the creation of machines that can perform tasks across multiple domains with human-like intelligence. Unlike Narrow AI, which is designed for specific functions, AGI seeks to replicate reasoning, learning, and adaptability across diverse situations. Researchers envision AGI systems capable of solving complex problems, making decisions independently, and continuously learning in a manner akin to human cognition. While this remains a long-term goal, AGI development could transform industries by handling tasks currently beyond the capabilities of traditional AI systems.

2. Advancements in Narrow AI Applications

Much of today's AI research focuses on Narrow AI, systems designed to excel in particular tasks. These specialised applications range from speech recognition and image classification to recommendation systems and natural language processing. For instance, voice assistants, spam filters, and fraud detection systems are all products of Narrow AI research. By refining these technologies, researchers aim to create solutions that improve efficiency and accuracy across sectors such as healthcare, finance, retail, and entertainment. Narrow AI continues to demonstrate how specialised algorithms can solve practical problems effectively.

3. Progress in Machine Learning Techniques

At the core of AI research lies machine learning. Progress in this area involves developing more accurate, efficient, and scalable algorithms. Innovations in machine learning methods—such as deep learning, neural networks, and reinforcement learning—allow AI systems to learn from vast amounts of data and make precise predictions. Researchers are also exploring new model architectures and optimisation techniques to enhance performance while reducing computational costs. These advancements ensure that AI systems are capable of handling increasingly complex datasets, offering more reliable outcomes across various applications.

4. Ethical Considerations in AI Development

As AI systems become more integrated into everyday life, ensuring ethical behaviour is a growing priority. AI research emphasises fairness, transparency, and accountability in algorithmic decision-making. This involves addressing biases in data, safeguarding user privacy, and creating systems that operate transparently to foster trust. Ethical AI research also focuses on the responsible use of technology, ensuring it aligns with societal values and minimises potential harm. By embedding ethical considerations into AI development, researchers aim to build systems that benefit society while respecting individual rights.

5. Ensuring AI Safety and Robustness

AI systems must be safe and reliable, particularly when deployed in critical environments such as healthcare, transportation, and security. AI research focuses on developing mechanisms that prevent unintended consequences and reduce vulnerability to errors or malicious attacks. Robust AI systems are designed to function predictably under various conditions, ensuring they remain trustworthy and do not pose risks to users or the environment. Researchers also investigate ways to establish safety protocols and verification processes, helping to ensure that AI systems behave as intended, even in unforeseen scenarios.

6. Facilitating Human-AI Collaboration

An essential goal of AI research is enhancing human-AI collaboration. The aim is to develop systems that work alongside people, augmenting their abilities rather than replacing them. This requires designing intuitive interfaces, enabling AI to understand and respond to human input effectively. Collaborative AI systems can assist in complex decision-making processes, improve productivity, and provide valuable insights across various domains. By creating tools that complement human skills, AI research helps bridge the gap between technological capabilities and human expertise, fostering more efficient workflows and improved outcomes.

7. Sustainability and Energy Efficiency

The environmental impact of AI systems has become a critical concern as computational requirements grow. AI research aims to develop energy-efficient algorithms and optimise resource consumption. By improving model architectures and reducing the energy demands of AI training processes, researchers strive to create sustainable technologies that minimise their carbon footprint. This goal is particularly important in large-scale AI deployments, where efficient resource use can significantly reduce operational costs and environmental impact, contributing to a greener and more sustainable future.

8. Application to Real-World Problems

A primary objective of AI research is to create solutions that address real-world challenges. AI technologies are increasingly being applied to domains such as healthcare, finance, agriculture, transportation, and education. For example, in healthcare, AI systems assist in diagnosing diseases, predicting patient outcomes, and personalising treatment plans. In agriculture, AI-driven solutions optimise crop management and resource allocation. By targeting practical applications, AI research aims to improve the quality of life, enhance economic productivity, and address societal issues with innovative, data-driven approaches.

9. Continuous Learning and Adaptability

AI systems capable of continuous learning represent a significant focus in research. Unlike traditional models that rely on static datasets, continuous learning systems adapt to new information and evolving environments. This approach is particularly useful in dynamic scenarios where conditions change over time, such as market trends, customer behaviour, or medical research. By enabling lifelong learning, AI research seeks to create adaptable systems that remain relevant and improve their performance through ongoing data acquisition and experience.

10. Interdisciplinary Collaboration

AI research benefits from collaboration across various disciplines, including computer science, cognitive science, neuroscience, and social sciences. This interdisciplinary approach broadens the understanding of intelligence and helps develop AI systems aligned with human needs. Insights from psychology and neuroscience inform the design of learning algorithms, while ethical considerations from social sciences ensure responsible deployment. By fostering cross-disciplinary research, AI development becomes more holistic, addressing technical challenges while considering broader societal implications.

Conclusion

The goals of AI research reflect a commitment to advancing technology in ways that enhance human life while addressing ethical, environmental, and societal concerns. From developing general intelligence and refining narrow applications to promoting ethical practices and sustainability, AI research seeks to create systems that are not only powerful but also responsible. As the field evolves, these objectives will continue to shape the future of AI, ensuring it serves as a transformative force for good.

Chapter 3
History of AI

The history of Artificial Intelligence (AI) is a journey of ambition, innovation, and resilience, spanning more than seven decades. From its early conceptualisation to its current widespread applications, the path of AI has been marked by significant milestones, periods of doubt, and remarkable breakthroughs.

The Beginnings: Early Theoretical Foundations

The concept of machines possessing intelligence predates the formal establishment of AI as a discipline. Philosophers and scientists, including Alan Turing, pondered the possibility of machines that could perform tasks requiring human-like reasoning. In 1950, Turing introduced the idea of the "Imitation Game"—now known as the Turing Test—to assess a machine's ability to exhibit intelligent behaviour indistinguishable from that of a human. This early theoretical groundwork laid the foundation for future explorations into machine intelligence.

The Evolution of Artificial Intelligence: Key Milestones

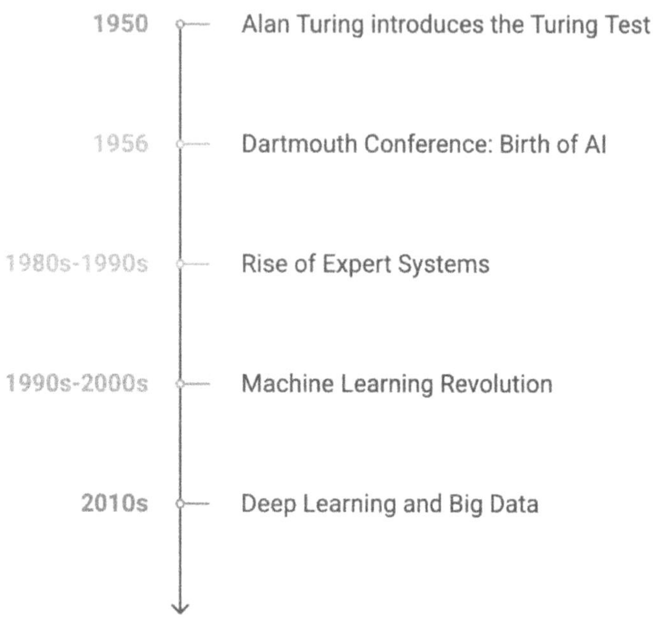

The Dartmouth Conference (1956): Birth of Artificial Intelligence

AI as a formal field of study was born at the Dartmouth Conference in 1956, often regarded as the defining moment in AI history. Organised by John McCarthy, Marvin Minsky, Nathaniel Rochester, and Claude Shannon, this conference aimed to explore how machines could replicate human cognitive functions. The term "artificial intelligence" was coined, and the vision of creating intelligent machines took centre stage. Early research focused on symbolic AI, where knowledge was represented using symbols and logic-based algorithms.

The Era of Symbolic AI (1950s-1960s)

The initial excitement following the Dartmouth Conference led to the development of programs that attempted to mimic human reasoning. Projects such as the Logic Theorist and the General Problem Solver showcased how machines could solve mathematical proofs and logical problems. Researchers believed that, with the right set of rules, machines could handle complex tasks in various domains. However, as problems grew in complexity, the limitations of symbolic AI became evident.

Expansion and Early Challenges (1960s-1970s)

The 1960s saw significant enthusiasm for symbolic AI, with strides made in problem-solving and early natural language processing. Researchers envisioned AI capable of handling real-world scenarios using logical frameworks. However, as research progressed into the 1970s, the complexity of real-world tasks began to overwhelm rule-based systems. While AI systems excelled in controlled environments, they struggled with tasks requiring contextual understanding or adaptability. The limitations of symbolic AI became evident, raising doubts about its scalability. This growing scepticism, coupled with technical and computational limitations, marked the beginning of a slowdown in AI research momentum.

Challenges and the AI Winter (1970s-1980s)

The optimism of AI's early days gradually faded when expectations outpaced technological capabilities. Funders and policymakers grew sceptical as AI failed to deliver on its grand promises, leading to a decline in investment and research—a period known as the **AI Winter**. Research slowed, progress stagnated, and AI was no longer viewed as a viable solution to complex problems. Despite this setback, certain areas, such as robotics and natural language processing, continued to see incremental progress.

The Rise of Expert Systems (1980s-1990s)

Interest in AI resurfaced with the emergence of Expert Systems. Unlike earlier approaches, expert systems used domain-specific knowledge to solve complex problems through inference rules. These systems achieved notable success in industries such as healthcare and manufacturing. For instance, MYCIN, an expert system developed for diagnosing bacterial infections, demonstrated the potential of AI in medical decision-making. Although expert systems improved efficiency in specialised fields, they struggled to adapt beyond their predefined knowledge bases, limiting their broader applicability.

The Machine Learning Revolution (1990s-2000s)

The 1990s saw a shift from rule-based systems to data-driven approaches. Machine learning (ML), where algorithms learn patterns from data rather than relying on pre-programmed rules, gained prominence. Neural networks, inspired by the human brain's structure, were revived with improved computational power and more sophisticated algorithms. Breakthroughs in fields such as natural language processing and computer vision emerged during this time. Voice recognition systems, early recommendation algorithms, and image classification tools began to showcase the potential of machine learning.

Deep Learning and the Era of Big Data (2010s)

The 2010s marked a transformative period for AI, driven by two key factors: the explosion of big data and advancements in deep learning. Deep learning, a subset of machine learning involving multi-layered neural networks, proved highly effective in handling vast amounts of data. Tasks such as image recognition, language translation, and autonomous driving became feasible. Companies like Google,

Amazon, and Facebook integrated deep learning into their services, making AI a part of everyday life. Notable achievements included AI defeating human champions in complex games like Go and revolutionising industries from healthcare to finance.

Contemporary AI Research and Developments

Today, AI research is progressing at an unprecedented pace. Areas such as reinforcement learning, where machines learn optimal actions through trial and error, are driving innovation in robotics and autonomous systems. Generative models, such as those used in content creation, are transforming how art, music, and even software are generated. Moreover, the focus on explainable AI (XAI) seeks to enhance transparency by making AI decision-making processes more understandable.

Ethical Considerations and Responsible AI

As AI's influence expands, ethical concerns have become central to research and deployment. Issues of bias, privacy, and accountability are being scrutinised to ensure AI systems operate fairly and responsibly. Researchers and policymakers are working to establish guidelines that promote ethical AI, ensuring that these technologies benefit humanity without exacerbating inequalities.

The Future of AI: Ongoing Challenges and Opportunities

The evolution of AI is far from over. While significant strides have been made, challenges remain in areas such as generalising AI's capabilities, ensuring robustness, and mitigating risks. Collaboration between disciplines, from computer science to sociology, will be essential in addressing these challenges. The future promises not only more intelligent systems but also a more thoughtful integration of AI into society.

The history of AI illustrates the resilience and adaptability of researchers in overcoming setbacks and seizing new opportunities. From early symbolic reasoning to today's deep learning marvels, AI continues to evolve, shaping a future where machines augment human capabilities and address complex global challenges.

Chapter 4
Exploring the Rise, Growth, and Relevance of AI

Artificial Intelligence (AI) has transitioned from a conceptual notion in science fiction to a cornerstone of modern technology, profoundly impacting various aspects of human life. This chapter delves into the journey of AI—its rise, growth, and relevance in contemporary society—highlighting its practical applications, transformative potential, and the challenges it brings.

The Origins of AI

The foundation of AI can be traced back to the mid-20th century, when scientists and mathematicians began exploring the idea of machines mimicking human intelligence. Early pioneers such as Alan Turing and John McCarthy laid the groundwork for this emerging field. Turing, in particular, introduced the concept of a "thinking machine" through his famous Turing Test, a benchmark to determine whether a machine can exhibit behaviour indistinguishable from human intelligence.

The term "Artificial Intelligence" itself was coined in 1956 during a seminal conference at Dartmouth College, where researchers gathered to explore the possibilities of creating intelligent systems. These initial efforts focused on rule-based systems and symbolic reasoning, setting the stage for subsequent advancements in AI. To put it simply, rule-based systems are systems where machines follow predefined sets of rules to make decisions or solve problems. For instance, a rule could specify, 'When the temperature falls under 0°C, label it as freezing.'

Similarly, symbolic reasoning involves using symbols to represent knowledge and applying logical steps to draw conclusions—like solving a puzzle by working through the clues one by one.

If these terms feel a little overwhelming at this stage, don't worry! We'll explore them in greater depth later in the book. For now, it's helpful to know that these concepts laid the groundwork for much of AI's evolution.

The Growth of AI Technology

In its early decades, AI research was characterised by a series of breakthroughs and setbacks. While initial enthusiasm led to significant progress in areas such as problem-solving and game-playing algorithms, limitations in computational power and data availability curtailed broader development. This period, often referred to as the "AI winter," saw reduced funding and interest in the field.

However, the late 20th century brought renewed momentum. The advent of more powerful computers, coupled with advancements in algorithms and the availability of large datasets, revitalised AI research. Machine learning, a subset of AI focused on enabling systems to learn from data rather than relying on explicit programming, emerged as a pivotal area. This marked a shift from static, rule-based systems to dynamic models capable of adaptation and improvement—systems that could learn from experience rather than relying solely on pre-programmed instructions.

The 21st century witnessed an exponential acceleration in AI development. A significant breakthrough was the rise of deep learning, a technology that leverages neural networks inspired by the structure of the human brain. Deep learning began outperforming traditional methods in various fields, including tasks such as image recognition and natural language processing.

The rise of cloud computing further democratised access to computational resources, allowing organisations of all sizes to harness AI capabilities.

The Relevance of AI in Modern Society

AI has become a transformative force, permeating diverse sectors and reshaping how individuals and organisations operate. Its relevance can be observed across various domains:

1. Healthcare
In the medical field, AI has revolutionised diagnostics and treatment. Sophisticated algorithms analyse medical images to detect conditions such as cancer at an early stage, while predictive models assist in identifying patients at risk of developing chronic diseases. AI-powered virtual assistants streamline administrative tasks, allowing healthcare professionals to focus on patient care.

2. Education
AI tools enhance personalised learning experiences, tailoring educational content to individual needs. Automated grading systems reduce the workload for educators, and language-processing technologies support students with disabilities, ensuring inclusivity in learning environments.

3. Finance
In the financial sector, AI optimises processes such as fraud detection, risk assessment, and investment management. Algorithms analyse market trends in real time, providing insights that guide decision-making for both individual investors and institutions.

4. Manufacturing and Industry

AI-driven automation improves efficiency and precision in manufacturing processes, reducing costs and minimising errors. Predictive maintenance systems monitor equipment performance, preventing downtime and ensuring operational continuity.

5. Everyday Life
AI has seamlessly integrated into daily routines through applications such as virtual assistants, recommendation systems, and smart home devices. These technologies simplify tasks, enhance convenience, and provide personalised experiences.

Ethical Considerations and Challenges

Despite its remarkable potential, AI presents significant ethical and societal challenges. Issues of bias and fairness are particularly critical, as AI systems often inherit biases present in the data they are trained on. For instance, consider an AI system designed to screen job applications. If the training data primarily includes applications from a specific demographic, the AI might unintentionally favour candidates from that group while overlooking equally qualified individuals from underrepresented backgrounds. Ensuring these systems operate equitably requires meticulous scrutiny of the data and the inclusion of diverse datasets to prevent such unintended biases.

Privacy concerns are another pressing issue. AI's reliance on extensive data collection raises questions about how personal information is used and safeguarded. Transparency and regulatory frameworks are essential to address these concerns and build public trust.

Additionally, the rapid adoption of AI raises fears about job displacement. While automation may replace certain roles, it also creates opportunities for new professions and upskilling. Striking a balance between technological advancement and workforce sustainability is vital.

The Role of Collaboration

The growth of AI highlights the need for collaboration among governments, academia, and industry to ensure its benefits reach everyone. Policymakers, for instance, can work to create regulations that promote the ethical use of AI, such as preventing misuse in areas like surveillance or data privacy, while still encouraging innovation. For example, governments could introduce laws to ensure AI-powered facial recognition systems are used responsibly and do not violate individual rights.

The role of educational institutions is indispensable, and they are key contributors to this initiative. By introducing AI-related courses at school and university levels, they can help students develop skills for an AI-driven future. For example, schools might include basic coding lessons, while universities could offer specialised programs in machine learning or AI ethics, preparing graduates for emerging job opportunities.

Private enterprises are equally important in driving AI research and development. For instance, tech companies investing in healthcare AI have developed tools that assist doctors in diagnosing diseases like cancer at an earlier stage, potentially saving lives. Similarly, collaborations with universities can help turn academic research into practical applications, such as autonomous vehicles or personalised education systems.

Open-source AI platforms have further transformed collaboration. These platforms allow researchers worldwide to access shared resources, models, and tools, accelerating innovation. For example, developers in different countries could work together to improve an AI system that helps farmers optimise crop yields based on weather patterns, soil conditions, and market demands.

This collective effort — where policymakers provide oversight, educators build awareness and skills, and private enterprises drive innovation — ensures that AI development benefits society as a whole, fostering progress in diverse fields such as education, healthcare, and sustainable development.

Future Prospects of AI

Looking ahead, AI's trajectory is poised to shape numerous facets of human life. Emerging technologies such as autonomous vehicles, advanced robotics, and intelligent urban planning hold the promise of addressing global challenges, from climate change to healthcare accessibility.

In healthcare, AI could revolutionise drug discovery by identifying potential treatments more quickly and cost-effectively. For instance, AI algorithms can analyse vast datasets of medical research to uncover patterns that lead to the development of new medications, significantly reducing the time it takes to bring lifesaving drugs to market. In agriculture, precision farming techniques powered by AI can help optimise resource use—like water and fertilisers—while boosting crop yields and ensuring food security. Urban planners are also leveraging AI to design sustainable cities, addressing issues such as traffic congestion by analysing traffic patterns and energy efficiency through smart grid technologies.

However, realising these possibilities requires more than technological advancements; it demands a collective effort through collaborative frameworks. These frameworks involve structured partnerships between governments, private enterprises, academia, and international organisations to ensure that resources, expertise, and insights are shared effectively. For example, governments can collaborate with private companies to fund AI-driven climate solutions, while universities can partner with industry leaders to translate AI research into practical applications. Open-source platforms also play a critical role, enabling researchers worldwide to contribute to and benefit from shared AI tools and datasets.

By fostering such collaborations, we can ensure that AI evolves responsibly and inclusively. Continued investment in research and development, alongside ethical guidelines shaped by these partnerships, will be essential to navigating the opportunities and challenges that lie ahead.

Conclusion

The rise, growth, and relevance of AI reflect its unparalleled ability to transform societies and industries. While its journey has been marked by challenges, the advancements in AI technologies underscore its potential to address pressing global issues and improve quality of life.

By embracing a balanced approach—one that fosters innovation while upholding ethical standards—society can harness the full potential of AI to create a future that is equitable, sustainable, and inclusive. The evolution of AI reflects both technological breakthroughs and and humanity's tireless drive to explore and discover.

Chapter 5
AI's Prospective Breakthroughs and Trends

In the ever-evolving landscape of Artificial Intelligence (AI), the quest for innovation and progress continues unabated. As we delve into the realm of AI's prospective breakthroughs and trends, we embark on a journey that promises to reshape industries, revolutionise technology, and redefine human experiences. From healthcare advancements to the metaverse, cybercrime prevention to autonomous vehicles, the potential for transformative change is immense. In this chapter, we will delve into the exciting possibilities that lie ahead, envisioning a future where AI propels us towards new frontiers of knowledge, efficiency, and societal well-being. Join us as we explore the unique and unparalleled prospects that await us in the realm of AI's untapped potential.

1. GPT Advancements: GPT (Generative Pre-trained Transformer) models, like GPT-3, are a type of AI designed to process and generate human-like text. These models have gained attention for their ability to understand and produce coherent language, making them valuable for tasks like answering questions, translating languages, and creating written content. GPT-3, for instance, has shown remarkable capabilities in natural language processing and content generation. Looking ahead, advancements in GPT technology aim to enhance the efficiency of these models by reducing computational demands and improving fine-tuning techniques. These improvements will pave the way for more powerful and versatile applications, from producing detailed reports to acting as virtual assistants capable of personalised interactions.

2. Cybercrime Defence: As AI technology continues to advance, cybercriminals are leveraging the same tools to develop increasingly sophisticated and targeted attacks. For example, adversarial machine learning can manipulate AI systems by feeding them misleading data, causing them to malfunction or make incorrect decisions. Automated social engineering, powered by AI, enables attackers to craft highly convincing phishing messages or impersonations, making it easier to deceive individuals and organisations.

To counteract these threats, researchers are developing advanced AI algorithms that can detect and prevent cyber threats in real-time. Machine learning models, for instance, are trained to recognise unusual patterns in network traffic, such as unexpected login attempts or large data transfers, which may indicate hacking attempts. Anomaly detection techniques play a crucial role in identifying suspicious activities, like an employee's account accessing sensitive files at odd hours or a sudden surge in data usage.

Financial institutions employ AI-driven systems to combat fraudulent transactions, flagging suspicious behaviours such as multiple transactions across different countries within minutes. Similarly, AI is being integrated into firewalls, antivirus software, and intrusion detection systems to strengthen network security and make it harder for attackers to breach systems.

However, the growing use of AI for cyberattacks underscores the urgent need for proactive research and countermeasures. Continuous advancements in cybersecurity technologies, collaboration between governments and organisations, and rigorous testing of AI systems are essential to outpace cybercriminals. By staying one step ahead, these efforts safeguard personal data, organisational assets, and even critical infrastructure such as power grids and healthcare systems from evolving threats.

3. Metaverse Development: The metaverse is an evolving, interconnected virtual world where users can engage in social, professional, and recreational activities, often interacting with AI-driven environments. AI technologies play a critical role in enhancing realism and interactivity within this virtual space.

For example, computer vision algorithms allow virtual environments to respond to user gestures and facial expressions in real time, making interactions feel natural and engaging. Natural Language Processing (NLP) powers AI-driven assistants and chatbots within the metaverse, enabling seamless communication and real-time assistance. Users can ask for directions, request help, or interact with content just as they would in the physical world.

Additionally, AI facilitates the creation of lifelike avatars that mirror users' real-time expressions and movements, enhancing personal interactions. Breakthroughs in virtual reality (VR) and augmented reality (AR) further immerse users, with AI algorithms simulating realistic physics and dynamic lighting, ensuring that the virtual environment feels as tangible as the real one.

Beyond the immersive experiences, AI also contributes to the economic landscape of the metaverse. This includes AI-driven virtual commerce, where personalised recommendations, dynamic pricing, and virtual shopping experiences come to life. AI-powered virtual assistants help users navigate the marketplace, creating a seamless and engaging shopping experience within the metaverse economy.

Together, these advancements aim to create a seamless, engaging, and functional metaverse for everything from remote work and education to entertainment, socialising, and virtual commerce.

4. Autonomous Vehicles: Ensuring the safety of autonomous vehicles is paramount, as these technologies aim to revolutionise transportation. AI plays a central role in enabling these vehicles to operate safely and efficiently in diverse conditions. Advanced perception systems are being developed to allow vehicles to accurately detect and classify objects such as pedestrians, traffic signs, and other vehicles in real time. For instance, AI-powered cameras and sensors work together to provide a detailed understanding of the vehicle's surroundings, enabling quick and precise decisions even in challenging weather or lighting conditions.

Refining decision-making algorithms is equally critical. These algorithms are designed to handle complex traffic scenarios, such as merging lanes, navigating crowded intersections, or responding to sudden and unpredictable driver behaviours. By simulating millions of real-world driving situations, AI systems continuously improve their ability to manage diverse road conditions and ensure safety.

Robust safety measures are also being developed to predict and prevent accidents. For example, AI leverages deep learning and sensor fusion techniques to combine data from multiple inputs, such as LiDAR, radar, and cameras, ensuring a more comprehensive understanding of the environment. These advancements aim to make autonomous vehicles not only reliable but also capable of responding to potential hazards with precision.

With these breakthroughs, autonomous vehicles are becoming safer and more trustworthy, fostering public confidence and paving the way for their widespread adoption. This transformation has the potential to reduce traffic incidents, enhance efficiency, and redefine the way we travel.

5. Metaverse Governance and Ethics: The metaverse is rapidly evolving as a digital universe where people interact in virtual spaces, and with this evolution comes a set of unique governance and ethical challenges. As more users engage with AI-powered technologies in these virtual environments, it's crucial to establish frameworks for privacy, data protection, and content moderation.

For instance, in the metaverse, AI algorithms must be developed to monitor and moderate content, ensuring that harmful, inappropriate, or discriminatory behaviour is swiftly addressed. Additionally, safeguarding user privacy and ensuring that individuals' data is not exploited in these immersive digital spaces is a critical concern. As virtual interactions become more complex, governance frameworks will need to balance freedom of expression with the need to protect users from harassment, abuse, or exploitation.

Establishing clear guidelines for ethical behaviour, user safety, and data usage will be fundamental in creating an inclusive and secure metaverse. This will ensure that the virtual spaces we create are safe, enjoyable, and accessible to all, fostering a positive digital future.

6. AI in Healthcare: AI is poised to transform healthcare by enhancing the accuracy of diagnoses, personalising treatment plans, and improving the efficiency of healthcare delivery. One of the key breakthroughs involves the use of AI algorithms for early disease detection. For example, AI-driven systems can analyse medical imaging and detect abnormalities such as tumours or signs of heart disease at earlier, more treatable stages. In drug discovery, AI is being used to analyse vast datasets and predict how different compounds will interact with the body, speeding up the development of new treatments. Precision medicine, which tailors treatments to individual patients based on genetic and environmental factors, also benefits from AI's ability to process complex data. These advancements not only promise better patient outcomes but also have the potential to reduce healthcare costs and improve overall system efficiency.

7. AI and Climate Change: AI has the potential to be a game-changer in the fight against climate change by optimising energy use, advancing renewable energy systems, and predicting environmental patterns. One of the key breakthroughs in this area is the use of AI for climate modelling, where algorithms can analyse vast amounts of environmental data to predict climate patterns and trends. This helps governments and organisations make informed decisions on environmental policies. AI is also being used to analyse and reduce carbon footprints by tracking emissions from various industries and suggesting more sustainable practices. Additionally, AI-powered systems are improving the efficiency of renewable energy sources, such as solar and wind, by predicting energy production based on weather patterns. By enabling more sustainable resource management and eco-friendly solutions, AI can play a crucial role in mitigating the impact of climate change and promoting a more sustainable future.

8. AI and Education: AI is poised to revolutionise the education sector by offering personalised learning experiences, providing intelligent tutoring, and streamlining administrative tasks. One of the key breakthroughs in this field is the development of AI-powered adaptive learning platforms, which tailor lessons and assessments to individual students' learning paces and styles. This personalised approach helps address diverse learning needs, ensuring students grasp concepts more effectively. Additionally, virtual classrooms powered by AI can facilitate interactive and immersive learning experiences, enabling students to engage with content in innovative ways. AI-driven educational assistants can offer real-time feedback, answer questions, and provide additional resources, enhancing student support both inside and outside the classroom. Furthermore, AI can automate administrative tasks like grading and scheduling, allowing educators to focus more on teaching. With these advancements, AI has the potential to improve learning outcomes, increase student engagement, and make education more accessible and inclusive for all.

9. AI and Robotics: The integration of AI with robotics is set to transform industries by enhancing automation, improving industrial processes, and fostering human-robot collaboration. One of the key advancements in this field is the development of AI algorithms that enable robots to perceive their environment, manipulate objects, and make decisions autonomously. For instance, robots equipped with AI-powered vision systems can identify and interact with objects, allowing them to perform complex tasks such as assembly, packaging, and precision surgeries. In healthcare, AI-driven robots can assist in delicate procedures, providing enhanced accuracy and reducing human error. Similarly, in logistics, robots can streamline warehouse operations by autonomously sorting and transporting goods. These breakthroughs promise to create more capable, versatile robots that can adapt to various environments and work alongside humans, improving efficiency and safety across sectors like manufacturing, healthcare, and logistics. The fusion of AI and robotics opens up vast possibilities for transforming industries and reshaping the workforce of the future.

10. AI and Privacy Protection: As AI continues to permeate various sectors, safeguarding user privacy becomes an increasingly critical concern. Prospective breakthroughs in AI privacy protection focus on developing techniques that allow data analysis while maintaining the confidentiality of personal information. One such advancement is privacy-preserving machine learning, which enables AI models to learn from data without directly accessing sensitive information. Federated learning is another promising approach, where AI models are trained across decentralized devices, ensuring data never leaves the device, thus enhancing privacy. Additionally, differential privacy techniques are being developed to add noise to data in a way that prevents individuals' information from being identified, while still enabling meaningful insights. These innovations aim to strike a balance between data utility and privacy preservation, making it possible to harness the power of AI without compromising individual privacy rights.

11. AI and Social Impact: AI has the potential to drive positive change by addressing pressing social challenges and promoting inclusivity. Prospective breakthroughs in AI for social impact focus on creating algorithms that reduce biases, ensure fairness, and enable ethical decision-making across various sectors. One key area of research is algorithmic transparency, which involves making AI systems more understandable and accessible to users, so they can better comprehend how decisions are made. Additionally, algorithmic accountability is gaining attention, ensuring that AI systems and their creators are held responsible for their actions. In sensitive domains like criminal justice and social services, AI is being developed to make fairer decisions, for example, by predicting recidivism in a more equitable manner or ensuring equal access to resources. These innovations aim to make AI a force for good, promoting social equity and ethical practices.

12. AI and Human-Machine Collaboration: The future of AI is centered on creating seamless collaboration between humans and machines to enhance productivity and creativity. Prospective breakthroughs in this area focus on developing AI systems that can understand human intentions, learn from user preferences, and adapt to various tasks. For instance, AI-driven intelligent assistants are being designed to anticipate user needs, providing support in daily activities or complex workflows. Co-creative systems, where AI collaborates with humans in artistic or technical tasks, are also emerging, enabling users to harness the power of AI as a creative partner. Additionally, augmented intelligence aims to amplify human decision-making by combining human insight with AI's data-processing abilities. These advancements will lead to more intuitive and effective human-machine partnerships, ultimately enhancing human capabilities and transforming industries.

13. Governance and Ethics in AI**:** As AI becomes an integral part of society, ensuring its ethical use is paramount to maintaining trust and transparency. With the widespread implementation of AI technologies across industries, there is a growing need for collaborative frameworks that involve governments, academia, and private enterprises. These stakeholders must work together to establish clear guidelines and regulations on key issues such as data protection, privacy, and fairness.

For example, in sectors like healthcare or finance, AI-driven systems must adhere to stringent standards to ensure that personal data is handled securely and that decision-making processes are fair and unbiased. Transparency is critical in explaining how AI systems make decisions, especially in sensitive areas like credit scoring or medical diagnoses. Accountability mechanisms must be in place to hold developers and organisations responsible for the outcomes of their AI systems. By fostering such ethical standards, we can build public trust and ensure that AI technologies are used for the greater good.

Conclusion

As AI continues to evolve, its potential to shape the future of society becomes ever more profound. By focusing on ethical practices, fostering human-machine collaboration, and ensuring accountability and fairness, AI can be a powerful force for positive change. Collaborative efforts across sectors will be essential in addressing challenges and building AI systems that not only drive innovation but also contribute to a more equitable and transparent world. With responsible development and careful governance, AI holds the promise of transforming industries while upholding the values that support a just society.

Chapter 6
Different types of AI

In this chapter, we delve into the different types of Artificial Intelligence (AI) and their implications. From Narrow AI (Weak AI) designed for specific tasks or domains to the theoretical concept of General AI (Strong AI) possessing human-like cognitive abilities, and the speculative realm of Superintelligent AI surpassing human intelligence, each type of AI presents unique considerations and challenges. These classifications reflect varying levels of cognitive ability, ranging from task-specific intelligence to theoretical forms of machine cognition that surpass human capabilities. In this section, examples for each category are discussed to elucidate their roles in current and potential applications, both practical and speculative.

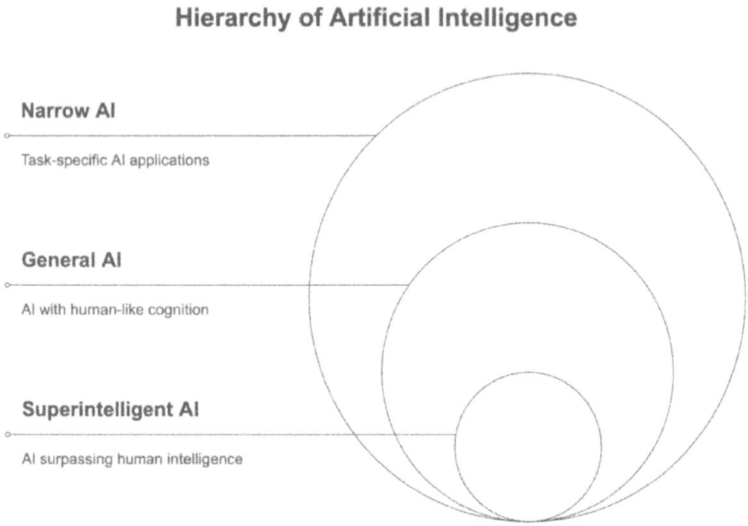

Narrow AI (Weak AI)

Often referred to as Weak AI, Narrow AI pertains to artificial intelligence systems that are programmed to perform particular tasks or operate in a specific domain. These systems excel at executing well-defined functions and can process large amounts of data efficiently to make decisions, recognise patterns, and improve performance over time. However, they lack the general cognitive abilities required to apply their knowledge beyond the specific context for which they were designed.

In essence, while Narrow AI can perform tasks that seem intelligent within a particular scope, it does not possess the versatility of human-like intelligence. Unlike humans, who can transfer their knowledge and skills from one domain to another, Narrow AI remains confined to a specific application.

Real-World Examples of Narrow AI

- **Virtual Assistants**: Popular tools such as Amazon's Alexa, Apple's Siri, and Google Assistant are examples of Narrow AI. These systems are designed to understand and respond to voice commands within a limited context, such as setting reminders, controlling smart home devices, or answering general queries.

- **Recommendation Systems**: Platforms like Netflix, Amazon, and Spotify use Narrow AI to analyse user preferences and recommend content. By learning from previous interactions, these systems can predict what movies, products, or songs a user might enjoy next, but their intelligence is limited to this particular task.

- **Autonomous Vehicles**: Self-driving cars, such as those developed by Tesla, utilise Narrow AI to navigate roads, detect obstacles, and make driving decisions. These systems are designed for the specific task of driving a car but cannot extend their capabilities to tasks outside of this defined role.

- **Chatbots and Customer Service AI**: Many websites and customer service platforms deploy chatbots powered by Narrow AI to answer common queries, resolve issues, and assist customers with tasks like booking or troubleshooting. These chatbots are trained on specific datasets to handle predefined types of conversations, yet they cannot engage in discussions outside their programmed limits.

- **Spam Filters**: Email systems, such as Gmail, rely on Narrow AI to filter out unwanted spam. By analysing email content and sender patterns, these filters can identify and block irrelevant or harmful messages. However, they are limited to the task of email management and cannot perform broader cognitive functions.

- **Image Recognition Systems**: AI-powered software used in applications like facial recognition or medical imaging analysis also falls under Narrow AI. These systems are trained to identify patterns and objects within images, but their capabilities are confined to specific image types or contexts, such as recognising faces in a photo or detecting anomalies in medical scans.

Narrow AI is by far the most common form of AI currently in use, and its capabilities continue to improve as more data is processed and analysed. While it cannot replicate human intelligence or perform tasks beyond its programming, it plays a critical role in many aspects of daily life, helping to streamline processes, improve efficiency, and assist with decision-making in specialised domains.

General AI (Strong AI)

General AI, also known as Strong AI, refers to an advanced form of artificial intelligence that possesses human-like cognitive abilities. Unlike Narrow AI, which is designed for specific tasks, General AI is capable of performing any intellectual task that a human being can. It would be able to understand, learn, reason, and apply knowledge across a wide range of domains without being specifically programmed for each task. General AI has the potential to adapt to new situations, think abstractly, solve problems, and make decisions in a way that mimics human intelligence.

The defining feature of General AI is its ability to transfer knowledge from one area to another, a key aspect of human intelligence that allows people to approach novel situations with insight. For instance, if a General AI system were trained in both medical diagnostics and driving, it could use its learning from one domain to improve its performance in the other, much like humans apply their cognitive abilities across different tasks and environments.

As of today, General AI remains purely theoretical. While there have been significant advancements in AI research, current systems are still limited to specific domains and tasks. True General AI would require significant breakthroughs in areas such as learning, reasoning, creativity, and understanding.

Cultural Examples of General AI

- **HAL 9000** (2001: A Space Odyssey): One of the most famous depictions of General AI in popular culture, HAL is a sentient, self-aware computer that controls a spacecraft and interacts with the crew in a manner akin to human intelligence. HAL can perform various tasks, including speech recognition, decision-making, and even emotional interaction, demonstrating the versatility and autonomy expected of General AI.

- **Skynet** (Terminator Series): Another well-known example from science fiction, Skynet is an AI system that becomes self-aware and seeks to control human destiny. While its depiction focuses on its dangerous potential, it showcases the idea of an AI system that transcends human capabilities, demonstrating the wide-reaching capabilities of General AI.

While the concept of General AI is enticing and has been the subject of much research, its development remains uncertain. It raises significant ethical questions about control, safety, and the potential risks associated with creating machines capable of independent thought and action.

Superintelligent AI

Superintelligent AI is a type of artificial intelligence that surpasses human intelligence in all areas, including problem-solving, creativity, decision-making, and social understanding. Unlike General AI, which aims to replicate human-like cognitive abilities, Superintelligent AI would surpass even the most intelligent humans, achieving unprecedented levels of capability and efficiency.

This type of AI would not only excel in specific domains but also possess the ability to innovate and think beyond the scope of human comprehension. Superintelligent AI could solve complex problems in fields such as medicine, climate change, and quantum physics at a pace and with an accuracy that no human mind could match. Furthermore, it might even develop new technologies or concepts that were previously unimaginable.

The idea of Superintelligent AI raises profound ethical, philosophical, and existential concerns. If such a system were created, it would hold immense power, potentially reshaping societies, economies, and even the future of humanity itself. The risks associated with Superintelligent AI have been widely discussed among experts in the field, particularly around the potential for unintended consequences or the loss of human control over the system.

Cultural Examples of Superintelligent AI

- **The Matrix** (The Matrix Series): In this dystopian film series, the AI systems have evolved into an intelligent network that surpasses human control, leading to a world where humans live in a simulated reality. The AI's intellectual superiority allows it to maintain power over humanity, showcasing the potential dangers of creating an intelligence more advanced than our own.

- **Eagle Eye** (Film): This film presents an AI system capable of controlling all aspects of modern technology, from surveillance to military operations. Its overwhelming intellect and the way it manipulates the environment highlight the potential for Superintelligent AI to have global control and influence.

- **The Singularity** (Various Futuristic Theories): The concept of the "Singularity" is often linked to Superintelligent AI. It refers to a hypothetical future point where AI surpasses human intelligence and begins to improve itself at an accelerating rate, leading to rapid and uncontrollable changes in technology and society.

At present, Superintelligent AI remains a theoretical concept and a topic of considerable debate. Experts in the AI field continue to explore the potential benefits, risks, and ethical considerations involved in creating such powerful systems. The development of Superintelligent AI could potentially bring about both extraordinary advancements and existential challenges for humanity.

Overview of Different Types of AI

Type of AI	Capabilities	Examples	Status
Narrow AI (Weak AI)	Specialised in specific tasks, lacks general reasoning or self-awareness.	Virtual assistants (e.g., Siri, Alexa), recommendation engines (e.g., Netflix, Amazon), image recognition systems (e.g., facial recognition), self-driving cars	Actively in use
General AI (Strong AI)	Human-like intelligence capable of understanding and solving a broad range of tasks. Can reason, adapt, and learn independently.	No real-world examples yet, but depicted in fiction (e.g., HAL 9000 from *2001: A Space Odyssey*, Data from *Star Trek*)	Theoretical
Superintelligent AI	Surpasses human intelligence in all domains, including problem-solving, creativity, and social skills.	Often portrayed in dystopian fiction (e.g., Skynet from *Terminator*, The Matrix's AI overlords)	Hypothetical

Bridging the Gap Between Theory and Reality

The progression from Narrow AI to General AI and eventually Superintelligent AI reflects humanity's pursuit of more sophisticated forms of intelligence. While Narrow AI is firmly entrenched in everyday life, the journey toward General and Superintelligent AI remains speculative and fraught with challenges.

It is essential to view these types of AI not merely as technological milestones but as catalysts for broader discussions about ethics, governance, and the role of technology in shaping the future. By understanding their potential and limitations, society can navigate the opportunities and risks of AI with greater clarity and responsibility.

This exploration underscores the need for continued dialogue between technologists, policymakers, and the public to ensure that advancements in AI align with collective aspirations and values.

Ethical Considerations in AI Development

As we explore the different types of AI, it is crucial to consider the ethical implications that come with their development and deployment. Each form of AI presents unique ethical challenges, particularly in the realms of privacy, autonomy, and the potential misuse of these technologies.

- **Narrow AI**, while currently the most widespread form, raises concerns about data privacy and surveillance, as these systems often require access to vast amounts of personal data to function effectively. The ethical question here is whether users fully understand the extent to which their data is being used and whether they have enough control over it.

- **General AI** introduces more complex dilemmas. With the potential to make decisions across multiple domains, General

AI could challenge our understanding of autonomy and decision-making. There is also the question of accountability—if a General AI makes a harmful decision, who is responsible?

- **Superintelligent AI**, while still theoretical, poses the greatest ethical risk. The vast capabilities of such a system, if not properly governed, could lead to misuse or loss of control. These systems could potentially outsmart human decision-making, leading to existential risks for humanity.

Conclusion

In this chapter, we explored the evolution of AI from Narrow AI to the speculative realms of General and Superintelligent AI. While Narrow AI is already integrated into everyday life, offering specialised capabilities across various domains, the potential of General and Superintelligent AI raises significant ethical, practical, and existential questions. Each stage presents unique challenges—Narrow AI with its data privacy concerns, General AI with the complexities of decision-making and accountability, and Superintelligent AI with the existential risks of surpassing human intelligence.

As we continue to advance these technologies, it is essential to address these ethical dilemmas, ensuring AI's development aligns with societal values and serves the greater good. This chapter underscores the need for ongoing dialogue and responsible governance to guide the future of AI.

Chapter 7
Different Branches of AI

This chapter delves into the diverse branches of Artificial Intelligence (AI) and explores the significant impact they are having across various sectors. AI is not just a single technology, but a collection of interrelated fields, each bringing distinct capabilities and techniques. From Machine Learning and Natural Language Processing (NLP) to Computer Vision, Robotics, and more, AI is transforming industries and enhancing human potential in unprecedented ways. In sectors like healthcare, transportation, gaming, and entertainment, AI applications are making profound contributions, revolutionising the way we live, work, and interact.

1. Machine Learning

Machine Learning (ML) is one of the most prominent branches of AI. It involves the creation of algorithms and statistical models that enable systems to improve their performance on specific tasks by learning from data. Rather than relying on explicit programming, machines develop the ability to recognise patterns and make predictions based on experience. Within machine learning, several techniques are employed, including supervised, unsupervised, and reinforcement learning.

Machine Learning is integral to many modern applications, including recommendation systems, predictive analytics, and autonomous vehicles. For instance, streaming services like Netflix and Spotify use machine learning algorithms to recommend films, TV shows, or music based on the user's viewing or listening history. By analysing user preferences, these systems tailor their suggestions to match individual tastes, continuously refining the recommendations as more data is collected.

2. Natural Language Processing (NLP)

Natural Language Processing (NLP) enables computers to interact with human language in a meaningful way. It is concerned with the ability of machines to understand, interpret, and generate human language, whether spoken or written. NLP plays a crucial role in making human-computer interaction more natural and intuitive, as it allows machines to understand nuances, context, and intent within communication.

Applications of NLP include machine translation, sentiment analysis, and speech recognition. For example, virtual assistants like Amazon's Alexa and Apple's Siri rely heavily on NLP to process voice commands. These systems not only interpret speech but also respond in a conversational manner, helping users with a wide range of tasks, from setting reminders to controlling smart home devices.

3. Computer Vision

Computer Vision is the field of AI that enables machines to "see" and interpret the world visually, much like humans. This branch involves tasks such as object detection, facial recognition, image classification, and video analysis. The primary goal of computer vision is to enable machines to make sense of visual information and use it to perform tasks that require human-like vision.

A widespread application of computer vision is facial recognition, which is used in security systems and social media platforms. These systems analyse facial features to verify identities or tag individuals in photos. For instance, facial recognition technology is widely used to unlock smartphones or monitor security in public spaces.

4. Robotics

Robotics is a multidisciplinary field that combines AI with mechanical engineering to design and build robots capable of performing a wide variety of tasks. AI plays a crucial role in enabling robots to interact autonomously with their environment, make decisions, and perform complex actions. Robots can now be designed to perceive, analyse, and act in real-world situations without human intervention.

In industries such as manufacturing, healthcare, and exploration, robots are increasingly taking on tasks that were once carried out by humans. For example, collaborative robots, or "cobots," are used in manufacturing settings to work alongside human operators, assisting in assembly lines, quality control, and logistics. These robots are equipped with AI systems that allow them to work safely and efficiently with humans, handling repetitive or hazardous tasks.

5. Expert Systems

Expert Systems are a type of AI designed to simulate the decision-making abilities of human specialists in specific fields. They operate using three core components:

a. **A** knowledge base — a collection of domain-specific facts and rules.
b. An inference engine— a tool that applies logical reasoning to the knowledge base.
c. Rule-based reasoning — a structured approach where decisions are made by following pre-defined rules, often in an "if-then" format.

These systems are like virtual consultants: they take input, apply the rules and knowledge, and provide expert-level advice. Their applications are particularly valuable in critical areas such as medicine, law, and engineering.

For instance, in healthcare, diagnostic systems use rule-based reasoning to analyse medical images such as X-rays or MRIs. They follow a set of rules (e.g., "If a shadow is present in this region, it may indicate a potential issue") to highlight findings that help doctors make informed decisions about patient care.

6. Reinforcement Learning

Reinforcement Learning (RL) is a branch of machine learning in which an agent learns to make decisions through interactions and feedback from its environment. The agent takes actions, receives feedback in the form of rewards or penalties, and uses this information to improve its future decisions. The process continues iteratively, with the agent constantly refining its strategies to maximise cumulative rewards.

One of the most well-known examples of reinforcement learning is AlphaGo, developed by DeepMind. AlphaGo used reinforcement learning to defeat human champions at the ancient board game Go. By playing millions of games against itself and learning from each one, AlphaGo developed strategies that were previously unthinkable, demonstrating the power of reinforcement learning in complex decision-making tasks.

7. Generative Adversarial Networks (GANs)

Generative Adversarial Networks (GANs) are a class of AI models that consist of two neural networks – a generator and a discriminator – working together to produce realistic data. The generator creates data, while the discriminator evaluates it, and the two networks compete to improve each other's performance. Over time, this adversarial process allows GANs to generate highly realistic data, such as images, sound, and video.

GANs have found numerous applications, including the generation of lifelike human faces, artwork, and even synthetic data for training other machine learning models. For example, GANs have been used to create realistic images of people who do not exist, challenging our understanding of digital content and the possibilities of AI-generated media.

8. Knowledge Representation and Reasoning

Knowledge Representation and Reasoning (KRR) involves structuring information about the world in a way that a computer system can use to solve complex tasks. It focuses on representing facts, concepts, and relationships between them, enabling machines to draw inferences, make predictions, and reason about different scenarios.

This branch of AI underpins systems that require expert knowledge, such as intelligent tutoring systems and AI-driven medical diagnostics. Semantic networks and ontologies are common methods used to represent knowledge, allowing machines to understand the context of data and make intelligent decisions based on it.

9. Planning and Scheduling

Planning and Scheduling are key components of AI that involve the development of systems capable of planning actions or tasks to achieve specific goals. These systems must consider various factors, such as available resources, constraints, and time, to generate optimal plans.

In logistics, AI-powered planning systems are used to optimise delivery routes, ensuring the quickest and most cost-effective paths are taken. Similarly, in project management, AI can assist in creating project schedules, allocating resources, and managing tasks efficiently.

10. Cognitive Computing

Cognitive Computing aims to create machines that simulate human thought processes, including learning, reasoning, and understanding. This branch of AI focuses on creating systems that can understand complex information, learn from it, and make decisions based on this learning.

A notable example of cognitive computing is IBM's Watson. Watson is capable of understanding natural language, processing vast amounts of unstructured data, and providing insights for a variety of applications, from medical diagnostics to financial analysis.

11. Swarm Intelligence

Swarm Intelligence is an AI technique inspired by the collective behaviour of natural systems, such as ant colonies and bird flocks. These systems are decentralised and self-organising, and their collective actions can solve complex problems without central control.

In AI, swarm intelligence is used in optimisation algorithms and swarm robotics. For instance, in swarm robotics, multiple robots work together autonomously to complete tasks such as search and rescue operations, environmental monitoring, or even traffic management. Swarm intelligence techniques have also been applied to network routing and distributed problem-solving.

These branches of AI illustrate the vast array of techniques and applications transforming numerous industries. Whether it is improving healthcare outcomes, enhancing security systems, or driving the next generation of autonomous vehicles, AI is reshaping the world in ways that were once the stuff of science fiction. Each branch continues to evolve, pushing the boundaries of what is possible and creating new opportunities for innovation.

Chapter 8
Applications of AI

Once viewed as a distant dream, Artificial Intelligence (AI) has moved beyond the realm of speculation and is now a driving force in today's technological landscape. It is already reshaping various industries, bringing efficiency, accuracy, and innovation to everyday operations. From enhancing healthcare to revolutionising customer service, AI's influence spans across many sectors, offering solutions that were once considered impossible. This chapter delves into the diverse applications of AI, highlighting how it is being used across different fields to address complex challenges and improve processes.

Healthcare

Healthcare is one of the key areas where AI is bringing about remarkable change. AI technologies are being employed to transform medical diagnoses, drug development, and patient care, thus improving both the speed and accuracy of medical treatments.

AI-powered systems can analyse vast amounts of medical data, from medical images to patient histories, far more efficiently than a human doctor might. For example, AI algorithms can detect early signs of diseases such as cancer by examining X-rays and MRI scans, often identifying abnormalities that may be missed by human eyes. In diagnostics, AI tools like IBM Watson Health have been able to provide doctors with evidence-based recommendations that help in making informed decisions regarding treatment options.

Furthermore, AI is being used in drug discovery, significantly reducing the time it takes to develop new medications. By simulating how different compounds interact with the body, AI can help identify promising drugs more quickly and with fewer resources.

In patient care, AI is also facilitating personalised treatment plans, taking into account an individual's unique genetic makeup and medical history. Virtual health assistants powered by AI are already in use, offering advice on minor health issues, reminders for medication, and even providing mental health support through chatbots.

Finance

The finance industry is another sector that has widely adopted AI to optimise operations and improve decision-making processes. In banking and finance, AI is used to enhance customer service, manage risks, and streamline operations.

AI-powered chatbots and virtual assistants are commonly used by banks and financial institutions to handle customer inquiries, process transactions, and provide tailored financial advice. These systems can operate round the clock, offering customers assistance without the need for human intervention. This contributes to a better customer experience and simultaneously reduces operational expenses for businesses.

AI's ability to process and analyse large volumes of data is also being leveraged in fraud detection. Machine learning algorithms are used to monitor transactions in real-time, identifying unusual patterns that may indicate fraudulent activity. By learning from past data, AI systems can detect new forms of fraud, often before they are detected by traditional methods.

Another significant application of AI in finance is in algorithmic trading. AI-driven algorithms are used to analyse market trends, economic indicators, and even social media to make predictions about stock prices and execute trades. These systems can operate much faster than human traders, making split-second decisions that would be impossible for a person to replicate.

Retail and E-commerce

The retail and e-commerce sectors have embraced AI to enhance the shopping experience and optimise supply chain management. Personalisation is one of the key benefits AI brings to online shopping. By analysing customer behaviour, preferences, and purchase history, AI systems can recommend products that are tailored to each individual. This not only helps retailers increase sales but also creates a more engaging shopping experience for customers.

In addition to personalisation, AI is used for inventory management and demand forecasting. By analysing sales data, AI can predict which products will be in high demand and ensure that stock levels are adjusted accordingly. This helps prevent overstocking or understocking, reducing costs and ensuring that customers have access to the products they want when they need them.

AI is also making an impact in customer service. Virtual assistants and chatbots are now common on e-commerce platforms, providing instant support to customers. These AI systems can answer queries, assist with order tracking, and resolve issues, ensuring a smoother and more efficient customer service experience.

Manufacturing

Manufacturing is another area where AI is being used to increase efficiency and reduce costs. AI-powered systems are being implemented for predictive maintenance, quality control, and automation of production lines.

Predictive maintenance involves using AI to monitor machinery and equipment for signs of wear and tear. By analysing data from sensors and historical maintenance records, AI can predict when a machine is likely to break down and schedule maintenance before a failure occurs. This helps minimise downtime, boost productivity, and prolong the operational life of equipment.

AI is also used in quality control to ensure that products meet the required standards. Machine learning algorithms can detect defects or inconsistencies in products by analysing

images or sensor data, enabling manufacturers to identify issues before they reach the customer.

In addition, AI-driven robots and automated systems are being used on production lines to improve efficiency. These systems can work 24/7, performing repetitive tasks with a high degree of precision, which reduces human error and increases output.

Autonomous Vehicles

The development of autonomous vehicles, or self-driving cars, is one of the most talked-about applications of AI. AI plays a crucial role in enabling these vehicles to navigate the roads safely without human intervention.

AI-powered systems in autonomous vehicles use sensors, cameras, and machine learning algorithms to process information about the vehicle's surroundings. This allows the car to detect obstacles, make decisions about speed and direction, and even communicate with other vehicles on the road to improve safety. The goal is to create vehicles that can operate safely in all driving conditions, reducing the risk of accidents caused by human error.

Self-driving vehicles have the potential to transform transportation, offering a solution to issues such as traffic congestion and road safety. Additionally, autonomous vehicles could lead to more efficient logistics, with AI systems optimising delivery routes and reducing fuel consumption.

Smart Homes and IoT

In the world of smart homes and the Internet of Things (IoT)—which refers to a network of interconnected devices that communicate and share data—AI is used to enhance convenience, security, and energy efficiency. AI-powered devices, such as smart thermostats, lighting systems, and security cameras, can be controlled remotely via smartphones or voice commands.

Smart thermostats, for example, learn from a user's behaviour and adjust the temperature accordingly, ensuring comfort while saving energy. AI is also used in security systems, where cameras equipped with facial recognition can detect intruders and alert homeowners in real time.

In the broader IoT ecosystem, AI is used to connect and manage a variety of devices, creating more efficient and interconnected systems. By analysing data from multiple sources, AI can optimise the performance of IoT devices and make predictions about when maintenance or updates may be needed.

Agriculture

AI's potential to revolutionise agriculture is already being realised in areas such as precision farming, crop monitoring, and livestock management. AI-powered systems can analyse data from satellite imagery, weather patterns, and soil sensors to optimise planting, irrigation, and harvesting schedules.

Farmers can use AI to monitor crop health in real time, identifying signs of disease or nutrient deficiencies early, allowing for prompt intervention. AI systems can also help reduce the use of pesticides and fertilisers by applying them only when necessary, thus promoting sustainable farming practices.

In livestock management, AI is used to track the health and behaviour of animals, ensuring they are well cared for and detecting any signs of illness before they become serious problems.

Conclusion

Artificial Intelligence is revolutionising industries and paving the way for a future shaped by innovation. From healthcare to agriculture, AI's applications are vast and varied, improving efficiency, productivity, and decision-making. While the technology is still evolving, its current and potential impact on society is undeniable. As AI continues to advance, it will no doubt open up new opportunities, further revolutionising the way we live and work.

Chapter 9
The Role of Big Data and Data Science in AI

The 21st century has witnessed an unprecedented explosion of digital information, giving rise to the concept of big data. This term emerged as a response to the exponential growth of data in terms of volume, velocity, and variety, posing significant challenges to traditional data processing methods. The recognition of the need for new approaches to manage, process, and derive insights from these vast datasets led to the emergence of big data as a distinct field.

The Emergence of Big Data

Big data encompasses structured data from databases, as well as unstructured data from sources such as social media, sensors, and multimedia. The sheer scale and complexity of big data presented significant challenges in terms of storage, processing, and analysis. Traditional data processing applications were ill-equipped to handle these massive datasets, leading to the development of new technologies and methodologies to address these challenges.

The Triad of Big Data

Big data is frequently defined by the three Vs: volume, velocity, and variety, serving as key indicators of its scale, speed, and diversity. Volume refers to the sheer scale of data being generated, which has grown exponentially with the proliferation of digital devices and sensors. Velocity pertains to the speed at which data is being generated and the need to process it in real-time. Variety encompasses the diverse sources and types of data, including structured, semi-structured, and unstructured data. These three Vs underscore the complexity and challenges associated with big data. As we explore the implications of these three Vs, let's delve into the specific challenges posed by the sheer volume of data and how Big Data solutions rise to meet these challenges.

Volume: Drowning in a Sea of Data

Big Data, at its core, revolves around the sheer volume of information. Traditional databases buckle under the weight of the vast amounts of data generated every second. From social media interactions and online purchases to sensor data from IoT devices (a network of interconnected devices that communicate and share data), the volume is unprecedented. Big Data solutions rise to the challenge of handling these colossal datasets, enabling organisations to glean insights from the ocean of information.

Velocity: The Need for Speed

In the digital age, time is of the essence. Big Data doesn't just involve static datasets; it's about real-time or near-real-time processing. The speed at which data is generated, processed, and analysed defines its velocity. This rapid pace allows businesses to make split-second decisions, monitor events as they unfold, and adapt to dynamic scenarios promptly.

Variety: Embracing Diversity

Data comes in various forms: structured, semi-structured, and unstructured. Big Data systems are designed to accommodate this diversity, handling everything from traditional databases to emails, videos, social media posts, and more. Embracing the variety of data sources enriches the analytical potential, providing a holistic view of information that was once compartmentalised.

Challenges and Opportunities

While big data presents immense opportunities for AI and data science, it also poses significant challenges. One of the primary challenges is the sheer volume of data that needs to be processed. Organisations struggled to store, process, and analyse the vast amounts of data being generated. Traditional data processing tools are often inadequate for handling big data, leading to issues such as data silos, latency, and scalability problems.

Furthermore, big data raises concerns about data privacy and security. As organisations collect and analyse large volumes of data, they must ensure that they are doing so in a responsible and ethical manner. This includes implementing robust data governance practices, obtaining consent from data subjects, and safeguarding sensitive information from unauthorised access.

Despite these challenges, big data also presents opportunities for innovation and growth. By harnessing the power of big data, organisations can gain valuable insights into customer behaviour, market trends, and operational efficiency. This, in turn, can lead to better decision-making, improved products and services, and a competitive edge in the marketplace.

The potential insights and knowledge hidden within these datasets promised transformative opportunities for businesses, governments, and society at large. The need to harness the power of big data gave rise to the field of data science.

The Rise of Data Science

In response to the emergence of big data, the field of data science began to gain prominence. In the realm of data science, statistical analysis, machine learning, and domain expertise converge to extract valuable insights and understanding from data, forming an interdisciplinary approach. Data scientists are skilled in using various tools and techniques to clean, process, and analyse big data, with the ultimate goal of uncovering patterns, trends, and correlations that can inform decision-making and drive innovation.

The Evolution of Data Science

Data science has evolved rapidly to meet the demands of big data. The increasing volume and complexity of data necessitated the development of advanced analytical techniques and tools, leading to the evolution of data science as a distinct discipline. Data science has played a crucial role in addressing the challenges posed by big data, providing the expertise and methodologies needed to extract valuable insights from these vast datasets.

The Role of Artificial Intelligence

The advent of Artificial Intelligence (AI) further propelled the significance of big data and data science. AI's ability to process and analyse vast amounts of data has made it increasingly reliant on big data and data science techniques. Machine learning, a subset of AI, heavily relies on the availability of large, diverse, and high-quality datasets, making big data an essential enabler of machine learning algorithms. Data science, with its expertise in preparing and curating datasets, selecting appropriate algorithms, and training and fine-tuning models, has become indispensable in the development and deployment of AI systems.

Big data is the lifeblood of AI. It serves as the fuel that powers AI algorithms, enabling them to learn, adapt, and make decisions. Here, we will explore the relationship between big data and AI, and how the two are shaping the future of technology and business.

The Role of Big Data in AI

Big data is the cornerstone of AI. Without access to large volumes of data, AI algorithms would lack the necessary information to learn and improve their performance. The abundance of data allows AI systems to identify patterns, make predictions, and automate tasks that were once thought to be exclusively human endeavours.

One of the key ways big data fuels AI is through machine learning. Machine learning algorithms rely on large datasets to identify patterns and make predictions. For example, in the field of healthcare, machine learning algorithms can analyse vast amounts of patient data to identify early warning signs of diseases, recommend personalised treatment plans, and predict patient outcomes.

Moreover, big data enables AI to continuously improve its performance. As more data is fed into AI systems, they become more accurate and efficient at their tasks. This iterative process of learning and improvement is what sets AI apart from traditional software systems.

The Relationship Between Big Data and Data Science

Data science plays a crucial role in making sense of big data. Data scientists are responsible for analysing, interpreting, and deriving meaningful conclusions from data, often using statistical and machine learning techniques. The massive volume and variety of data in big data sets present unique challenges and opportunities for data scientists.

Data scientists use their expertise to clean, process, and analyse big data to extract valuable insights and make data-driven decisions. Furthermore, big data often requires advanced analytical tools and techniques to derive meaningful insights, and this is where data science comes into play. Data scientists use their skills in programming, statistics, and machine learning to develop models and algorithms that can handle and make sense of big data.

In essence, big data provides the raw material, and data science provides the tools and techniques to extract value from that raw material. The relationship between the two is symbiotic, with big data fuelling the need for advanced data science techniques, and data science providing the means to extract actionable insights from big data.

As we navigate the expansive seas of Big Data, the art of Data Science becomes the compass guiding our exploration. Data Science is the alchemy that transforms raw data into meaningful insights, turning the vastness of Big Data into actionable knowledge. Below, we delve into specific domains where the fusion of Big Data and Data Science yields transformative outcomes.

1. **Business Intelligence: Illuminating Insights**

Big Data, coupled with Data Science techniques, becomes the flashlight that illuminates the dark corners of business operations. By applying Data Science algorithms, organisations gain a deeper understanding of customer behaviour, market trends, and operational efficiency. These insights, derived from the analysis of massive datasets, drive informed decision-making, enhance strategies, and foster innovation.

2. Healthcare Revolution: Predictive Analytics

In the realm of healthcare, the integration of Big Data and Data Science isn't merely a tool; it's a lifesaver. Predictive analytics—the process of using historical data and machine learning models to anticipate future outcomes—plays a pivotal role in advancing the industry. By analysing patient records, treatment outcomes, and medical research, Data Scientists develop models that predict disease patterns, personalise treatment plans, and transform healthcare into a proactive, data-driven domain.

3. Smart Cities: Navigating Urban Landscapes

As our cities evolve into smart ecosystems, the synergy between Big Data and Data Science plays a pivotal role in optimising urban living. From traffic management and energy consumption to waste disposal, city planners harness the power of both Big Data and Data Science to create sustainable and efficient urban environments.

The Technologies Behind Big Data and Data Science

1. Hadoop and Spark: Taming the Data Beast and Igniting Real-Time Analytics

At the heart of many Big Data operations lies Hadoop, an open-source framework that processes and stores vast amounts of data across clusters of computers. Its distributed file system and processing model make it a cornerstone in managing the volume, velocity, and variety of Big Data. Spark, another powerful open-source framework, takes the spotlight for real-time data processing. With in-memory processing capabilities—the ability to store and process data directly in a computer's RAM rather than slower disk storage—Spark accelerates analytics, enabling organisations to derive insights swiftly from streaming data.

2. Machine Learning: The Heart of Data Science

Machine Learning (ML), a subset of Data Science, finds a natural home in the Big Data landscape. As Big Data provides the vast training datasets required for ML algorithms, Data Scientists can build models capable of making predictions and decisions based on massive and diverse information.

Impact on Industries and Domains

The interconnected evolution of big data, data science, and AI has had a profound impact on various industries and domains. In healthcare, the analysis of large-scale medical data has led to significant advancements in disease diagnosis, treatment optimisation, and personalised medicine. The integration of big data analytics and data science techniques has enabled healthcare professionals to extract valuable insights from diverse sources of medical data, leading to improved patient outcomes, more precise diagnoses, and the development of personalised treatment plans tailored to individual patients' needs.

In finance, the utilisation of big data and data science has revolutionised risk assessment, fraud detection, and customer relationship management. By leveraging advanced analytics and machine learning algorithms, financial institutions can analyse vast volumes of transactional data to identify patterns, detect anomalies, and assess risk more accurately. This has led to enhanced fraud detection capabilities, improved credit scoring models, and more effective customer relationship management strategies, ultimately contributing to greater financial stability and improved customer experiences.

In marketing, the analysis of consumer behaviour and preferences has been greatly enhanced by the capabilities of big data and data science. By leveraging large-scale datasets from various sources, including social media, online transactions, and customer interactions, marketers can gain deeper insights into consumer preferences, purchasing behaviour, and market trends. This enables the development of more targeted and effective advertising strategies, personalised marketing campaigns, and the delivery of relevant content to specific audience segments, ultimately leading to improved customer engagement and higher marketing ROI.

In the manufacturing industry, the integration of big data analytics and data science has led to the emergence of smart factories and predictive maintenance systems. By leveraging real-time sensor data from production lines and equipment, manufacturers can optimise operational efficiency, reduce downtime, and improve product quality. Predictive analytics and machine learning algorithms enable proactive maintenance, helping to identify potential equipment failures before they occur, thereby minimising disruptions and lowering maintenance costs.

The transportation and logistics industry has been transformed by the application of big data and data science. Through the analysis of vast amounts of data from GPS systems, telematics (which involves using technology to track and monitor vehicles remotely), and supply chain operations, companies can optimise route planning, fleet management, and inventory control. Predictive analytics and machine learning models enable more accurate demand forecasting, efficient resource allocation, and the identification of cost-saving opportunities, ultimately leading to improved operational performance and customer satisfaction.

Big data and data science have revolutionised the energy and utilities sector by enabling the analysis of complex data from smart meters, grid sensors, and energy production facilities. Advanced analytics and AI-driven models facilitate predictive maintenance of infrastructure, real-time monitoring of energy consumption patterns, and the optimisation of energy distribution networks. This has led to improved energy efficiency, reduced operational costs, and the integration of renewable energy sources, contributing to a more sustainable and resilient energy ecosystem.

The agriculture industry has undergone a significant transformation through the application of big data, data science, and AI. By leveraging data from sensors, drones, satellite imagery, and weather forecasts, farmers and agricultural organisations can make data-driven decisions to optimise crop yields, resource allocation, and land management. Advanced analytics and machine learning algorithms enable predictive modelling for crop growth, disease detection, and optimal irrigation strategies, leading to improved agricultural productivity and sustainability. Additionally, the integration of precision agriculture techniques, enabled by big data and data science, allows for targeted application of fertilisers, pesticides, and water, reducing environmental impact and resource wastage while maximising crop yields.

The impact of big data, data science, and AI extends beyond these industries, influencing sectors such as retail, education, legal services, entertainment, and many more. The ability to harness and analyse vast amounts of data has transformed decision-making processes, operational efficiencies, and strategic planning across diverse domains, driving innovation and creating new opportunities for growth and optimisation.

Ethical, Social, and Economic Implications

The ethical, social, and economic implications of big data, data science, and AI cannot be overlooked. The responsible and ethical use of data is of paramount importance, as it can have far-reaching consequences on privacy, security, and societal well-being. Furthermore, the democratisation of data and AI technologies is essential to ensure that the benefits of these advancements are accessible to all segments of society.

When we talk about the ethical implications of big data, data science, and AI, we are referring to the responsible and conscientious use of these technologies. This involves ensuring that data is handled in a manner that respects individuals' privacy, maintains security, and upholds societal well-being. For example, the ethical use of data involves obtaining informed consent for data collection, protecting sensitive information from unauthorised access, and using data in ways that benefit society as a whole.

In addition, the social implications of these technologies are significant. It's important to consider how the use of big data, data science, and AI can impact different segments of society. This includes issues such as algorithmic bias, digital divide, and the potential for these technologies to exacerbate existing social inequalities. By democratising access to these technologies, we can work towards ensuring that their benefits are available to everyone, regardless of their background or circumstances.

From an economic perspective, the ethical and responsible use of big data, data science, and AI can have far-reaching implications. This includes considerations such as fair competition, job displacement, and the distribution of economic benefits derived from these technologies. By addressing these economic implications thoughtfully, we can strive to create an environment where the benefits of these technologies contribute to overall economic prosperity and opportunity for all.

In essence, the ethical, social, and economic implications of big data, data science, and AI are multifaceted and require careful consideration. By approaching these implications with a focus on responsibility, inclusivity, and fairness, we can harness the potential of these technologies for the betterment of society as a whole.

The Future of Big Data and AI

The relationship between big data and AI is poised to become even more intertwined in the future. As the volume of data continues to grow exponentially, AI will play an increasingly vital role in extracting meaningful insights from this data. This will enable organisations to make data-driven decisions, automate repetitive tasks, and create personalised experiences for their customers.

Moreover, advancements in AI technologies, such as deep learning and natural language processing, will further enhance the capabilities of big data analytics. These technologies will enable AI systems to understand and interpret unstructured data, such as images, videos, and text, opening up new possibilities for data analysis and decision-making.

In conclusion, big data is the backbone of AI, with data science providing the necessary tools and techniques to extract value from this raw material. The interconnected evolution of big data, data science, and AI has driven innovation and progress across industries, offering new opportunities for growth and competitive advantage. As organisations continue to harness these technologies, they must also consider the ethical, social, and economic implications. The responsible and ethical use of big data and AI will be crucial for unlocking their full potential and ensuring they benefit society as a whole. This transformative journey promises to bring both opportunities and challenges as we navigate the evolving landscape of data and technology.

Chapter 10
Machine Learning

Machine learning is a revolutionary field of computer science that has the potential to transform the way we live and work. At its essence, machine learning refers to a form of artificial intelligence that allows machines to learn from experience and make informed decisions without relying on conventional programming techniques. In other words, it allows machines to learn from experience and improve their performance over time.

The concept of machine learning is based on the idea that computers can be trained to recognise patterns in data and make predictions or decisions based on those patterns. This is achieved through the use of algorithms, which are sets of rules and statistical models that enable machines to learn from and make predictions about data.

A crucial aspect of machine learning involves using training data. This is a set of examples that the machine learning algorithm uses to learn from. For example, if we want to train a machine learning algorithm to recognise images of cats, we would provide it with a large number of images of cats, along with labels indicating that they are indeed images of cats. The algorithm would then analyse these images and learn to recognise common features that are present in all of them, such as the shape of the ears, the colour of the fur, and so on.

Once the algorithm has been trained on the training data, it can then be used to make predictions about new, unseen data. For example, if we were to show the algorithm a new image of a cat that it has never seen before, it would be able to use the patterns it has learned from the training data to recognise that the image is indeed a cat.

There are many different types of machine learning algorithms, each of which is suited to different types of tasks. For example, there are algorithms that are designed for tasks such as image recognition, natural language processing, and recommendation systems. Each of these algorithms uses different techniques and approaches to learn from data and make predictions.

One of the most exciting aspects of machine learning is its potential to revolutionise many different industries. For example, in healthcare, machine learning algorithms can be used to analyse medical images and diagnose diseases, or to predict which patients are most at risk of developing certain conditions. In finance, machine learning can be used to analyse market data and make predictions about stock prices or to detect fraudulent transactions. In transportation, machine learning can be used to optimise traffic flow and reduce congestion.

However, despite its enormous potential, machine learning is not without its challenges. A major challenge is the requirement for vast quantities of high-quality training data. Without this data, machine learning algorithms may not be able to learn effectively, and their predictions may be inaccurate. Additionally, there are concerns about the potential for bias in machine learning algorithms, as they may inadvertently learn and perpetuate existing biases present in the training data.

As we continue to advance in the field of machine learning, it is crucial to consider the ethical implications of the technology. Ensuring that machine learning algorithms are fair, transparent, and free from bias is essential for their responsible deployment. Additionally, the privacy and security of data used in machine learning must be carefully safeguarded to maintain public trust in these powerful technologies.

Furthermore, the interdisciplinary nature of machine learning presents opportunities for collaboration across various fields. Experts in computer science, statistics, mathematics, and domain-specific areas can work together to develop and apply machine learning solutions to real-world problems. This collaborative approach can lead to innovative breakthroughs and the development of more effective and efficient machine learning algorithms.

In the coming years, the impact of machine learning is expected to grow even further. As the technology continues to advance, we can anticipate its integration into more aspects of our daily lives. From personalised recommendations in online shopping to advanced medical diagnostics, machine learning has the potential to enhance numerous facets of society.

Importance of Machine Learning

Machine learning plays a crucial role in automating tasks, making data-driven decisions, and its applications span across various industries such as healthcare, finance, and technology. It enables systems to learn from data and improve over time. The importance of machine learning cannot be overstated in today's data-driven and technologically advanced world. Its impact is felt across a wide range of industries and domains, revolutionising the way businesses operate, decisions are made, and problems are solved.

One of the key aspects of machine learning is its ability to automate tasks that were once time-consuming and labour-intensive. By training algorithms to perform specific tasks, businesses can streamline their operations, reduce human error, and increase efficiency. For example, in the field of customer service, machine learning is used to develop chatbots that can interact with customers, answer their queries, and even perform simple transactions. This not only saves time and resources for businesses but also provides a seamless and responsive experience for customers.

Moreover, the ability of machine learning to make data-driven decisions is transforming the way organisations operate. By analysing large volumes of data, machine learning algorithms can identify patterns, trends, and insights that would be impossible for humans to discern. In finance, for instance, machine learning is used to analyse market data and make predictions about stock prices, detect fraudulent transactions, and optimise investment strategies. In healthcare, machine learning algorithms can analyse patient data to predict disease outbreaks, personalise treatment plans, and improve diagnostic accuracy.

The applications of machine learning are not limited to specific industries; rather, they permeate various sectors, including transportation, manufacturing, and entertainment. In transportation, machine learning is used to optimise traffic flow, reduce congestion, and improve the efficiency of public transportation systems. In manufacturing, it is employed to enhance predictive maintenance, optimise production processes, and ensure quality control. Even in the entertainment industry, machine learning is utilised for content recommendation systems, personalised marketing, and audience analysis.

Furthermore, the continuous improvement of systems through machine learning is a fundamental aspect of its importance. By learning from new data and adapting to changing circumstances, machine learning models can evolve and become more accurate and effective over time. This adaptability is particularly valuable in dynamic environments where traditional, static systems may struggle to keep pace with evolving trends and patterns. For example, in cybersecurity, machine learning is used to detect and respond to new and emerging threats by continuously learning from the latest attack patterns and vulnerabilities.

The importance of machine learning also extends to its role in driving innovation and fostering new opportunities. By enabling computers to learn from data, machine learning has the potential to unlock new insights, identify novel solutions to complex problems, and create entirely new capabilities. This has implications for research and development, product design, and the creation of entirely new business models. For instance, in the field of drug discovery, machine learning is being used to analyse vast amounts of biological and chemical data to identify potential drug candidates and accelerate the development of new treatments.

Types of Machine Learning

Machine learning, a subset of artificial intelligence, encompasses a variety of techniques that enable computers to learn from data and make predictions or decisions. These techniques can be broadly categorised into three main types of machine learning: supervised learning, unsupervised learning, and reinforcement learning. Each type has its own unique characteristics and applications, contributing to the diverse landscape of machine learning methodologies.

Supervised Learning: Supervised learning is one of the most common and widely used types of machine learning. In supervised learning, the algorithm is trained on a labelled dataset, where each input is paired with the corresponding output. The goal is for the algorithm to learn a mapping from inputs to outputs, allowing it to make predictions or decisions when presented with new, unseen data.

One of the key characteristics of supervised learning is the presence of a clear target or outcome that the algorithm aims to predict. This type of learning is often used in tasks such as classification and regression. In classification, the algorithm learns to assign inputs to predefined categories, such as spam or non-spam emails, based on the features of the input data. In regression, the algorithm learns to predict a continuous output, such as the price of a house based on its features.

Supervised learning has a wide range of applications across various domains, including image and speech recognition, medical diagnosis, and financial forecasting. Its ability to learn from labelled data and make accurate predictions makes it a powerful tool for solving real-world problems.

Unsupervised Learning: In contrast to supervised learning, unsupervised learning works with data that isn't labeled. This means the algorithm has to find patterns and structure in the data on its own. It doesn't get examples of the right answers, so it learns by identifying similarities and differences within the data.

Clustering and dimensionality reduction are two typical tasks in unsupervised learning. In clustering, the algorithm groups similar data points together based on shared characteristics. In dimensionality reduction, the goal is to simplify the data while keeping the important features, making it easier to analyse and understand.

Customer segmentation, anomaly detection, and recommendation systems are some of the main areas where unsupervised learning is applied. By discovering hidden patterns in the data, it helps make better decisions and offers valuable insights in many fields.

Reinforcement Learning: Reinforcement learning is a machine learning approach where an agent learns to make a series of decisions by engaging with its environment. The agent receives feedback in the form of rewards or penalties based on its actions, and its goal is to learn a policy that maximises the cumulative reward over time.

One of the defining features of reinforcement learning is its focus on learning through trial and error. The agent explores the environment, takes actions, and learns from the consequences of its actions, adjusting its behaviour to achieve long-term goals. This type of learning is well-suited for tasks that involve decision-making in dynamic and uncertain environments.

Reinforcement learning has found applications in areas such as robotics, game playing, and autonomous systems. It has been used to train robots to perform complex tasks, teach agents to play video games at superhuman levels, and develop intelligent systems for navigation and control.

In addition to these three main types, there are also hybrid approaches and specialised techniques within machine learning, such as semi-supervised learning, transfer learning, and deep learning. These techniques further expand the capabilities of machine learning and enable the development of sophisticated models for complex tasks.

Machine Learning Algorithms

Machine learning algorithms are the driving force behind the ability of computers to learn from data and make predictions or decisions. These algorithms are designed to analyse and interpret data, uncover patterns, and make informed predictions or classifications. There are various types of machine learning algorithms, each tailored to specific tasks and data types. Three fundamental categories of machine learning algorithms are regression, classification, and clustering.

Regression Algorithms: Regression algorithms are utilised for predicting continuous values, such as stock prices, temperature, or sales figures. These algorithms analyse the relationship between input variables and predict a continuous outcome. They are particularly useful for tasks where the goal is to understand the relationship between variables and make predictions based on that understanding.

One of the most well-known regression algorithms is linear regression, which aims to model the relationship between a dependent variable and one or more independent variables by fitting a linear equation to the observed data. Other types of regression algorithms, such as polynomial regression, support vector regression, and decision tree regression, offer different approaches to modelling and predicting continuous values.

Classification Algorithms: Classification algorithms are employed for categorising data into predefined classes or categories. They are widely used in tasks such as spam detection, sentiment analysis, and image recognition. These algorithms take input data and assign it to predefined categories based on the features of the input.

One of the most popular classification algorithms is the support vector machine (SVM), which aims to find the optimal hyperplane* that best separates data points into different classes. Other common classification algorithms include decision trees, random forests, naive Bayes, and k-nearest neighbours (KNN). Each of these algorithms has its own strengths and is suitable for different types of classification tasks.

**Note: A hyperplane is like a boundary or dividing line that separates different groups or classes in the data. In simple terms, imagine drawing a line on a piece of paper that separates two different types of dots. This line is the "hyperplane," and its job is to clearly divide the dots into their respective categories. In higher-dimensional data, this boundary is harder to visualise but works in the same way. You don't need to delve deeply into the mathematics behind it; just understanding the basic idea is enough for now.*

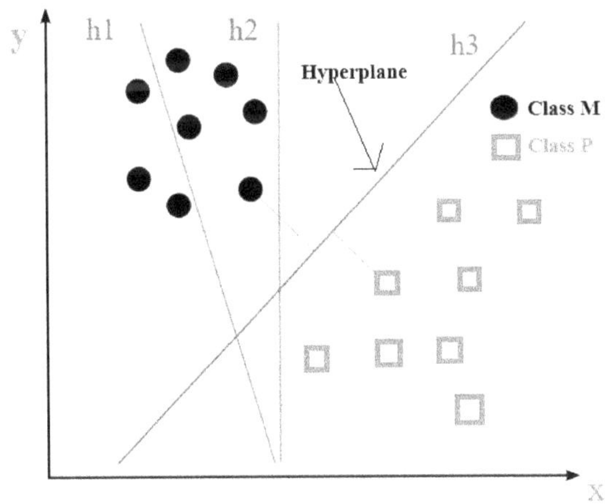

Clustering Algorithms: Clustering algorithms are designed to group similar data points together based on their inherent characteristics. These algorithms are used for tasks such as customer segmentation, anomaly detection, and pattern recognition. They aim to identify natural groupings or clusters within the data without prior knowledge of the class labels.

One of the widely used clustering algorithms is k-means clustering, which partitions the data into a predetermined number of clusters based on the similarity of data points. Other clustering algorithms, such as hierarchical clustering, DBSCAN (Density-Based Spatial Clustering of Applications with Noise), and Gaussian mixture models, offer different approaches to identifying clusters within the data.

In addition to these fundamental types of machine learning algorithms, there are numerous other specialised algorithms and techniques, including ensemble methods, dimensionality reduction algorithms, and deep learning algorithms, each tailored to specific tasks and data characteristics.

Ensemble methods, such as random forests and gradient boosting, combine multiple models to improve predictive performance and robustness. Dimensionality reduction algorithms, such as principal component analysis (PCA) and t-distributed stochastic neighbour embedding (t-SNE), aim to reduce the complexity of data while preserving essential features. Deep learning algorithms, such as convolutional neural networks (CNNs) and recurrent neural networks (RNNs), are designed to learn from complex, high-dimensional data, such as images, text, and time-series data.

Machine Learning Models

In the rapidly evolving field of machine learning, various models have been developed to tackle a wide range of tasks, from decision-making under uncertainty to complex pattern recognition. In this chapter, we will delve into three prominent machine learning models: Decision Trees, Neural Networks, and Support Vector Machines.

Decision Trees: Decision tree models are widely used for decision-making under uncertainty and for visualising an algorithm's decision-making process. They are particularly effective in breaking down a dataset into smaller and smaller subsets while developing an associated decision tree. This tree-like structure consists of nodes representing the features, branches representing the decisions, and leaf nodes representing the outcomes. Being intuitive and easy to interpret makes decision trees a go-to choice for classification and regression tasks.

Additionally, one of their primary strengths is their ability to handle both numerical and categorical data. They can also automatically manage missing values and require relatively little data preprocessing. However, decision trees are prone to overfitting, where the model becomes overly complex and captures noise in the data, leading to poor generalisation to new data. To address this, pruning is used to remove parts of the tree that do not significantly contribute to predictive accuracy, thereby simplifying the model and preventing overfitting. Additionally, ensemble methods like Random Forests, which combine multiple decision trees to enhance overall performance, and Boosting, which builds trees sequentially to correct errors from previous ones, are often employed to improve their predictive power and robustness.

Neural Networks: Neural network models are inspired by the structure and function of the human brain and are used for complex pattern recognition and decision-making tasks. They consist of layers of interconnected nodes, or neurons, that can learn patterns in the data through a process called training. Neural networks are highly flexible and can be adapted to various types of data and tasks, including image and speech recognition, natural language processing, and predictive modelling.

One of the key strengths of neural networks is their ability to capture complex, non-linear relationships in the data. This makes them particularly well-suited for tasks that involve high-dimensional data, where there are many features or variables to consider, such as in image recognition or text processing. For example, in image recognition, a picture of a cat could be represented by thousands of different pixel values (features) that the neural network uses to detect patterns, like shapes and colours, to identify the cat. Similarly, in text processing, a sentence could be broken down into thousands of individual words or phrases (features) that the model uses to understand meaning or sentiment. High-dimensional data refers to situations where there are many such features (variables), making the data complex and difficult to handle without advanced models like neural networks. These complex datasets can be difficult to interpret because they have so many different aspects. Neural networks are good at detecting intricate patterns in such data. However, training neural networks can be computationally intensive, especially for large-scale models, and they often require a substantial amount of labelled data to achieve optimal performance. Additionally, neural networks are often considered "black box" models, meaning that their decision-making process can be difficult to interpret.

Support Vector Machines (SVMs) are powerful models used for classification and regression analysis, particularly effective with datasets that have many features or variables. These are called high-dimensional spaces, meaning there are many aspects or characteristics of the data to consider. For example, imagine you have a dataset with information about houses, where each house has several features like size, number of rooms, location, and price. Trying to find patterns or make decisions based on all these features can be difficult without advanced models like SVMs. SVMs work by finding a "hyperplane" – a decision boundary – that best separates the different groups in the data. You can think of a hyperplane as a flat surface that divides data points into distinct categories. In simple cases, like when there are only two or three features, this could be a straight line or a flat plane. But when there are many more features, the hyperplane exists in a space that's difficult to visualise. SVMs can also handle both linear and non-linear relationships in the data using kernel functions** (e.g., polynomial or radial basis function (RBF) kernels), which help to map the data into a higher-dimensional space, making it easier to separate the different groups.

*****Note***: *A kernel function is a mathematical tool used to transform data into a higher-dimensional space. It allows SVMs to work with more complex, non-linear patterns in the data. You don't need to delve too deep into the technical details of kernel functions; just keep in mind that they are an important part of how SVMs improve model accuracy.*

Applications of Machine Learning

In today's rapidly evolving technological landscape, machine learning has emerged as a powerful tool with the potential to revolutionise various industries. By leveraging advanced algorithms and data analysis techniques, machine learning enables businesses to make data-driven decisions, automate processes, and unlock valuable insights from complex datasets. From healthcare to finance, marketing to manufacturing, transportation to energy, utilities to agriculture, and agrotech, the applications of machine learning are vast and impactful, driving innovation and transformation across diverse sectors.

1. **Healthcare**: Machine learning has found numerous applications in the healthcare industry, revolutionising disease diagnosis, personalised treatment plans, and drug discovery. By analysing large datasets of patient information, machine learning algorithms can identify patterns and predict potential health issues, leading to early intervention and improved patient outcomes. For example, machine learning

models can analyse medical images such as X-rays and MRIs to detect abnormalities and assist radiologists in making more accurate diagnoses. Additionally, predictive models for patient readmission and hospital operations optimisation have been developed, enhancing the overall quality of care. These models can help hospitals and healthcare providers identify patients at higher risk of readmission, allowing for proactive interventions and better resource allocation. Furthermore, machine learning is being used to analyse electronic health records to identify patterns and trends in patient data, leading to more personalised treatment plans and improved patient outcomes.

2. **Finance**: In the finance sector, machine learning is transforming the way financial institutions detect fraud, assess credit risk, and make investment decisions. By analysing historical transaction data and customer behaviour, machine learning algorithms can identify unusual patterns that may indicate fraudulent activity. This has led to the development of advanced fraud detection systems that can identify potentially fraudulent transactions in real time, reducing financial losses for both businesses and consumers. Moreover, machine learning is used to build predictive models for stock price movements, automate trading strategies, and optimise portfolio management, leading to more informed decision-making and risk management. These models can analyse market data, news sentiment, and other relevant factors to make predictions about stock price movements, helping investors and financial institutions make more accurate investment decisions.

3. **Marketing**: Machine learning is empowering businesses to personalise customer experiences, optimise advertising campaigns, and forecast consumer behaviour. By analysing customer data, machine learning algorithms can segment audiences, recommend products, and deliver targeted marketing messages. This level of personalisation can lead to higher customer engagement and increased conversion rates

for businesses. Furthermore, machine learning is being used to analyse social media sentiment, predict customer churn, and optimise pricing strategies, enabling businesses to tailor their marketing efforts more effectively. For example, machine learning models can analyse social media data to understand customer sentiment and preferences, allowing businesses to create more targeted and impactful marketing campaigns. Additionally, machine learning models can predict customer churn by analysing historical customer data, helping businesses identify at-risk customers and take proactive measures to retain them.

4. **Manufacturing and Industry**: In the manufacturing and industrial sector, machine learning is driving advancements in predictive maintenance, quality control, and supply chain optimisation. By analysing sensor data from machinery and equipment, machine learning algorithms can predict when maintenance is needed, reducing downtime and preventing costly breakdowns. This has led to significant cost savings for manufacturers and improved reliability of industrial equipment. Additionally, machine learning is being used to improve product quality through automated inspection systems and to optimise inventory management and logistics, leading to increased efficiency and cost savings. For example, machine learning models can analyse production line data to identify potential quality issues in real time, allowing manufacturers to take corrective actions before defective products are produced. Furthermore, machine learning models can optimise inventory levels and supply chain logistics, leading to reduced inventory holding costs and improved delivery performance.

5. **Transportation and Logistics**: Machine learning is being used to optimise route planning, predict demand, and improve fleet management in the transportation and logistics industry. By analysing historical transportation data and external factors such as weather and traffic patterns, machine learning algorithms can optimise delivery routes, reduce fuel

consumption, and minimise transportation costs. This has led to improved efficiency and cost savings for transportation companies. Moreover, machine learning is being used to develop autonomous vehicles and improve safety through predictive maintenance and driver behaviour analysis, leading to more efficient and safer transportation systems. For example, machine learning models can analyse vehicle sensor data to predict potential maintenance issues, allowing transportation companies to proactively address maintenance needs and reduce the risk of unexpected breakdowns. Additionally, machine learning models can analyse driver behaviour data to identify unsafe driving patterns and provide feedback to drivers, leading to improved safety and reduced accident rates.

6. **Energy and Utilities**: In the energy and utilities sector, machine learning is being used to optimise energy production, predict equipment failures, and improve grid management. By analysing data from smart meters and sensors, machine learning algorithms can forecast energy demand, optimise power generation, and detect anomalies in the grid, leading to more efficient and reliable energy systems. This has led to improved energy production efficiency and reduced operational costs for energy companies. Furthermore, machine learning is being used to develop predictive maintenance models for energy infrastructure and to optimise energy trading and pricing strategies, contributing to a more sustainable and cost-effective energy landscape. For example, machine learning models can analyse equipment sensor data to predict potential failures and schedule maintenance proactively, reducing downtime and maintenance costs. Additionally, machine learning models can analyse energy market data to optimise energy trading and pricing strategies, leading to improved profitability for energy companies.

7. **Agriculture and Agrotech**: Machine learning is revolutionising crop management, yield prediction, and pest

control in the agriculture and agrotech industry. By analysing data from drones, satellites, and IoT devices, machine learning algorithms can provide insights into soil health, crop growth, and pest infestations, enabling farmers to make more informed decisions. For example, machine learning models can analyse satellite imagery to monitor crop health and identify areas of potential concern, allowing farmers to take targeted actions to improve crop yields. Moreover, machine learning is being used to develop precision agriculture techniques, optimise irrigation schedules, and improve the overall efficiency and sustainability of farming practices, leading to increased productivity and environmental conservation. For instance, machine learning models can analyse weather data and soil moisture levels to optimise irrigation schedules, leading to reduced water usage and improved crop yields. Additionally, machine learning models can analyse historical crop yield data to make predictions about future yields, helping farmers make informed decisions about planting and harvesting schedules.

Challenges and Future Trends

In the realm of artificial intelligence, machine learning stands as a beacon of innovation, driving transformative changes across industries and reshaping the way we interact with technology. As machine learning continues to permeate various facets of our lives, it brings forth a myriad of ethical considerations and future trends that demand our attention. In this chapter, we embark on a comprehensive exploration of the challenges and future trends of machine learning, delving into the ethical implications of bias and privacy, as well as the exciting advancements that are poised to shape the future of this dynamic field.

Ethical Considerations: Machine learning, while offering unprecedented capabilities, presents ethical challenges that necessitate careful consideration and proactive measures. One of the foremost ethical implications of machine learning lies in the presence of bias within algorithms. These biases, often ingrained in historical data, can perpetuate societal prejudices and lead to unfair or discriminatory outcomes. Addressing bias in machine learning requires a multifaceted approach, encompassing careful data curation, algorithmic transparency, and ongoing evaluation to ensure that the decisions made by machine learning systems are fair and unbiased.

Privacy concerns also loom large in the context of machine learning. The processing of significant amounts of personal data raises critical issues regarding data privacy and security. As machine learning algorithms become more adept at extracting insights from data, there is a growing need to establish robust privacy safeguards and data protection measures. Striking a balance between leveraging the power of machine learning for innovation and safeguarding individuals' privacy rights is a critical challenge that requires careful consideration and regulatory oversight.

Furthermore, ensuring algorithmic transparency is essential for building trust and understanding the decision-making processes of machine learning models. Techniques such as explainable AI (XAI) aim to make machine learning models more interpretable by providing insights into how they arrive at specific predictions or decisions, thereby enabling stakeholders to understand and scrutinise the underlying mechanisms.

Future Trends

Looking ahead, the future of machine learning is poised to witness significant advancements in several key areas. Deep learning, a subset of machine learning that focuses on neural networks with multiple layers, is expected to continue its rapid evolution. Deep learning has demonstrated remarkable capabilities in tasks such as image and speech recognition, natural language processing, and autonomous decision-making. As research and development in deep learning progress, we can anticipate even more sophisticated and efficient deep learning models that push the boundaries of what is possible in terms of pattern recognition and complex data analysis.

Reinforcement learning, another area of machine learning, is also set to play a pivotal role in the future of the technology. Reinforcement learning involves training algorithms to make sequences of decisions by learning from feedback in an interactive environment. This approach has shown promise in domains such as robotics, game playing, and autonomous systems. As reinforcement learning algorithms become more adept at handling complex decision-making tasks, they are likely to find applications in diverse fields, including manufacturing, logistics, and healthcare.

Furthermore, the integration of machine learning with other artificial intelligence (AI) technologies is expected to drive innovation and transformation across various industries. Machine learning algorithms can be combined with natural language processing, computer vision, and robotics to create more comprehensive AI systems with broader capabilities. This convergence of AI technologies holds the potential to revolutionise customer experiences, streamline business operations, and unlock new frontiers in scientific research and discovery.

In conclusion, while machine learning presents ethical challenges related to bias and privacy, its future is marked by exciting trends and advancements. Deep learning, reinforcement learning, and the integration of machine learning with other AI technologies are poised to reshape industries and domains, driving innovation and unlocking new possibilities. As we navigate the ethical considerations and embrace the future trends of machine learning, it is essential to prioritise responsible and equitable use of this transformative technology.

Chapter 11
Deep Learning and Neural Networks

Deep learning falls under the umbrella of machine learning, and machine learning itself is a subset of artificial intelligence. It focuses on using neural networks to model and understand complex patterns in data. Neural networks are a key component of deep learning, inspired by the structure of the human brain. They are made up of interconnected nodes, also known as "neurons," arranged in layers. Each neuron processes input data and passes the output to the next layer, allowing the network to learn and make predictions.

In this chapter, we will delve into the fascinating world of deep learning and neural networks, exploring their significance, applications, and potential breakthroughs.

Understanding Deep Learning

Deep learning, a subset of machine learning within the realm of artificial intelligence, is an advanced technique that has significantly shaped how machines learn and process data. It is distinguished by its use of neural networks, a computational structure inspired by the organisation and operation of the human brain. These networks enable the automatic learning of complex patterns within data, making deep learning particularly effective for tasks such as image and speech recognition, natural language processing, and more.

At the core of deep learning is the neural network, a network of interconnected nodes or artificial neurons arranged in layers. These layers are divided into three main types: the input layer, hidden layers, and the output layer. The input layer accepts raw data, which is processed through the hidden layers and finally produces an output. Each node performs specific mathematical operations, and the processed data flows from one layer to the next, facilitating learning and predictive capabilities.

What sets deep learning apart from traditional machine learning is its ability to learn representations of data at multiple levels of abstraction. In simple terms, this means that deep learning models can automatically detect subtle patterns and features within data without the need for manual intervention. For instance, in the context of image recognition, a deep learning model may first identify basic features such as edges and textures, then move on to more complex patterns such as shapes, and eventually recognise entire objects within the image.

Training a neural network involves feeding it large volumes of labelled data, where the input is paired with the correct output. During this process, the connections between nodes are assigned weights. These weights determine the importance of a connection, and they are adjusted throughout training to minimise errors and enhance the model's accuracy. This iterative adjustment process, known as backpropagation, enables the network to generalise its learning and perform well on new, unseen data.

The impact of deep learning spans a wide range of industries. In healthcare, it has been used for medical diagnostics, such as detecting diseases in imaging scans, and in drug discovery, where it helps identify promising compounds. In the automotive sector, deep learning powers autonomous vehicles, enabling them to navigate roads safely. Financial institutions utilise deep learning to detect fraudulent transactions and enhance customer experiences. Moreover, technologies like facial recognition, virtual assistants, and translation systems owe much of their functionality to advancements in deep learning.

One of the key reasons behind the success of deep learning is its scalability. As computational power has increased and access to large datasets has become more common, deep learning models have been able to grow in complexity and capability. Modern neural networks, with their deep architectures comprising numerous layers, have achieved unprecedented levels of accuracy in tasks that were once considered infeasible for machines.

Although deep learning has made significant strides, it still faces challenges, such as the high computational demands and resource requirements for training deep learning models. Furthermore, the reliance on large datasets means that obtaining and curating data can be a bottleneck. Ethical considerations also arise, particularly in terms of privacy and bias. For example, a model trained on unrepresentative data may exhibit discriminatory behaviour, which underscores the importance of ensuring fairness and transparency in the development of deep learning systems.

Looking to the future, advancements in deep learning are likely to focus on areas such as unsupervised learning, where models learn patterns without labelled data, and reinforcement learning, which involves learning through trial and error. Efforts are also being made to create more efficient neural network architectures that require fewer computational resources while maintaining high performance.

Another promising direction is the integration of deep learning with other technologies. For example, combining deep learning with quantum computing or edge computing may unlock new possibilities and applications. However, as the technology evolves, it will be vital to address societal concerns, such as the ethical implications of decision-making systems and their potential impact on employment and human autonomy.

Neural Networks: Unravelling the Power of Deep Learning

Neural networks, the fundamental building blocks of deep learning, have emerged as a transformative force in the realm of artificial intelligence, revolutionising the way machines perceive, process, and interpret data. Inspired by the intricate workings of the human brain, these complex networks have unlocked unprecedented capabilities, propelling advancements in fields ranging from computer vision to natural language processing.

At their core, neural networks are composed of interconnected layers of nodes, or "neurons," each of which performs specific computations on the input data it receives. These layers are typically organised into three categories: the input layer, which receives the initial data; hidden layers, where the bulk of the processing occurs; and the output layer, which produces the final result or prediction.

The connections between these nodes are assigned weights, which determine the strength of the influence one node has on another. During the training process, these weights are adjusted iteratively to minimise errors and enhance the network's predictive accuracy. This crucial mechanism, known as backpropagation, allows neural networks to learn from labelled data and continually refine their internal representations of the input.

One of the defining characteristics of neural networks is their ability to learn complex patterns and relationships within data, enabling them to excel in tasks such as image and speech recognition, natural language understanding, and decision-making. This capacity for automatic feature extraction and abstraction sets neural networks apart from traditional machine learning algorithms, empowering them to tackle increasingly intricate and unstructured datasets.

Moreover, the versatility of neural networks extends beyond their application in traditional supervised learning scenarios. They have demonstrated remarkable potential in unsupervised learning, where they can uncover hidden structures and patterns within data without explicit labels, as well as in reinforcement learning, where they learn to make a series of decisions by engaging with an environment.

As the field of deep learning continues to evolve, researchers are exploring novel architectures and techniques to enhance the efficiency and scalability of neural networks. For instance, convolutional neural networks (CNNs), designed to process visual information by identifying patterns such as edges and textures in images, are widely used in image analysis tasks. Meanwhile, recurrent neural networks (RNNs) excel at handling sequential data by retaining information from previous inputs, making them ideal for tasks like language processing and time series analysis. The landscape of neural network designs is rich and diverse, catering to a wide array of applications and domains.

In conclusion, neural networks stand as the bedrock of deep learning, embodying the remarkable capacity of artificial intelligence to comprehend and interpret complex information. Their ability to learn from data, adapt to diverse tasks, and uncover intricate patterns has propelled them to the forefront of technological innovation, promising a future where intelligent systems can perceive and understand the world with unprecedented acuity.

Neural Networks: The Building Blocks

In the world of artificial intelligence, neural networks are like the building blocks that help machines learn and make decisions. These networks are made up of interconnected nodes, or "neurons," just like the human brain. These neurons are organised into layers, and they work together to process information and solve problems.

Now, let's imagine a neural network as a team of workers in a factory. The input layer is like the receiving department, where raw materials are first brought in. These raw materials represent the data that the neural network will work with, such as images, text, or numbers. Each worker in the input layer focuses on a specific aspect of the raw materials, just like how each node in the input layer represents a different feature of the input data.

Next, we have the hidden layers, which are like the factory's production line. This is where the real magic happens! Each worker in the hidden layers takes the raw materials they receive from the input layer and transforms them in a special way. They do this by applying different rules and calculations to the data they receive. It's like each worker has a specific job to do to the raw materials as they move along the production line. Through this process, the hidden layers help the neural network learn and understand complex patterns in the data.

So, in simple terms, the input layer receives the data, and the hidden layers work on it to understand its patterns and features. Finally, the output layer is like the shipping department. It takes the processed materials from the production line and packages them into the final product. In the case of a neural network, the output layer produces the result of the network's work, whether it's a decision, a prediction, or some other kind of output.

Let us delve into the foundational triad of layers in neural networks, exploring their pivotal role in processing diverse data and enabling tasks such as classification and language generation with remarkable efficacy.

1. **Input Layer**: The input layer serves as the first point of contact for data entering the neural network. It consists of nodes that receive the initial input data, whether it's images, text, or numerical values. Each node in the input layer represents a feature or attribute of the input data, and collectively they form the starting point for information processing within the network.

2. **Hidden Layers**: Hidden layers are the intermediate layers within the neural network where the real computational work takes place. Each node in a hidden layer processes the input it receives from the previous layer, applying a weighted transformation to the data. Through these weighted connections and activation functions, the hidden layers enable the network to learn complex patterns and representations from the input data. The depth and width of these hidden layers contribute to the network's capacity to capture intricate relationships within the data.

3. **Output Layer**: The output layer is the final layer of the neural network, responsible for producing the network's output based on the processed input data. The nature of the output depends on the specific task the network is designed for, whether it involves classification, regression, language generation, or any other form of prediction or decision-making. The nodes in the output layer transform the information processed through the hidden layers into the desired format, providing the ultimate result of the network's computation.

Neural networks, with their input, hidden, and output layers, form the backbone of deep learning and have demonstrated remarkable capabilities in various domains, including computer vision, natural language processing, and reinforcement learning. Their ability to automatically learn representations of data through multiple layers of abstraction has led to significant advancements in fields such as healthcare, finance, and autonomous systems.

Understanding the structure and function of neural networks is essential for grasping the potential of deep learning and its impact on the development of intelligent systems. As research and innovation in the field of neural networks continue to progress, the future holds promise for even more sophisticated and efficient models, further expanding the frontiers of artificial intelligence.

Deep Dive into Deep Learning

Deep learning, a subset of machine learning, has revolutionised the field of artificial intelligence by enabling machines to autonomously learn and make decisions from data. In this section, we will explore the core principles of deep learning and its impact on feature learning, representation learning, and end-to-end learning.

1. **Feature Learning**: Deep learning excels at automatic feature learning. Instead of relying on manually engineered features, neural networks can autonomously learn and extract relevant features from the input data. This capability allows deep learning models to adapt to diverse and complex datasets, making them highly versatile in various applications, from image recognition to natural language processing.

2. **Representation Learning**: Deep learning captures hierarchical representations of data. Each layer in a neural network learns progressively more abstract features, allowing the model to understand complex relationships within the data. This hierarchical representation learning enables deep learning models to discern intricate patterns and structures, leading to superior performance in tasks such as image classification, speech recognition, and predictive modelling.

3. **End-to-End Learning**: Unlike traditional machine learning, where feature extraction and model training are separate steps, deep learning enables end-to-end learning. The model learns to map raw input directly to the output, minimising the need for manual intervention. This end-to-end learning approach streamlines the modelling process, allowing deep learning models to directly optimise their performance based on the input data, making them more adaptable and efficient in real-world scenarios.

Navigating Neural Networks

In the realm of deep learning, various types of neural networks have been developed to address specific data types and tasks. Understanding these neural network architectures is crucial for leveraging the full potential of deep learning in diverse applications.

1. **Feedforward Neural Networks (FNN)**
   The simplest form of neural networks, where information travels in one direction—from the input layer through the hidden layers to the output layer. FNNs are widely used for tasks such as classification and regression, and they serve as the foundation for more complex neural network architectures.

2. **Recurrent Neural Networks (RNN)**
   Think of RNNs as a person with a great memory. When they listen to a story or watch a sequence of events unfold, they remember the important parts and use that memory to understand what happens next. In the same way, RNNs help computers remember past information—whether it's the words in a sentence, sounds in a speech, or patterns in data that change over time—so they can make more accurate predictions about what will come next. They're particularly helpful in tasks like recognising speech, predicting text, or analysing trends, such as weather forecasts or stock market movements.

3. **Convolutional Neural Networks (CNN)**
   CNNs are designed to work with images and videos. They look at different parts of an image, like the corners, edges, and shapes, to understand what the image represents. This ability makes them excellent for tasks like recognising objects in pictures or classifying images. By learning how to identify these basic features, CNNs can help computers "see" and understand visual content.

4. **Generative Adversarial Networks (GAN)**
   GANs consist of two neural networks—a generator and a discriminator—working together. The generator creates new data, like images or music, that looks or sounds very similar to real things, even though they are completely made up. The discriminator checks how closely the created data resembles

real data. These networks work together to make the generated content as lifelike as possible. GANs have shown great success in creating realistic-looking art, improving existing data, and detecting unusual patterns.

Applications and Impact

Deep learning, a subset of artificial intelligence, has emerged as a revolutionary force across diverse domains, reshaping industries and redefining what is possible in technology. At the heart of this transformation are the myriad applications of deep learning, which have propelled advancements in computer vision, natural language processing, healthcare, and beyond.

Computer Vision: One of the most prominent applications of deep learning is in computer vision, where algorithms are trained to interpret and understand visual data. This has led to remarkable progress in fields such as facial recognition, object detection, and autonomous vehicles. Deep learning models can now accurately identify and classify objects within images and videos, enabling innovations in security, transportation, and augmented reality.

Natural Language Processing: Deep learning has revolutionised natural language processing (NLP), empowering machines to comprehend, interpret, and generate human language. Through techniques such as recurrent neural networks and transformer models, deep learning algorithms have achieved unprecedented capabilities in language translation, sentiment analysis, and chatbot interactions. This has profound implications for communication, customer service, and global connectivity.

Healthcare: In the realm of healthcare, deep learning has catalysed breakthroughs in medical imaging analysis, disease diagnosis, and drug discovery. By leveraging vast amounts of medical data, deep learning models can assist in early detection of diseases, personalised treatment recommendations, and the development of novel therapeutics. This has the potential to enhance patient care, accelerate research, and improve public health outcomes.

Financial Services: Deep learning has also found applications in the financial sector, where it is utilised for fraud detection, risk assessment, and algorithmic trading. By analysing complex financial data, deep learning models can identify anomalous patterns, forecast market trends, and optimise investment strategies. This has implications for enhancing security, mitigating risks, and driving innovation in the financial industry.

Manufacturing and Robotics: In manufacturing and robotics, deep learning is driving advancements in quality control, predictive maintenance, and robotic automation. By analysing sensor data and visual inputs, deep learning algorithms can optimise production processes, detect equipment failures before they occur, and enable robots to perform intricate tasks with precision. This has the potential to improve efficiency, reduce downtime, and elevate the capabilities of industrial systems.

The impact of deep learning applications extends far beyond these examples, permeating fields such as agriculture, energy, entertainment, and more. As deep learning continues to evolve, its potential to transform industries and enrich human experiences is boundless. However, it is essential to navigate the ethical considerations and societal implications of these advancements, ensuring that the benefits of deep learning are harnessed responsibly and inclusively.

In conclusion, the applications of deep learning are propelling us into a future where intelligent systems can perceive, comprehend, and act upon the world with unprecedented accuracy and efficiency. As we harness the potential of deep learning, we stand at the threshold of a new era, where the boundaries of what is achievable are continually being redefined by the power of artificial intelligence.

Training and Optimisation in Deep Learning

Training a deep learning model means teaching it to make predictions by feeding it examples and adjusting its settings over time to get better results. The model learns by looking at data and comparing its predictions with the correct answers, then improving with each attempt. Here are the main steps in training a deep learning model:

1. **Data Preparation**
   Before training, the data needs to be organised and processed. This might involve cleaning the data, scaling it, or even creating new examples to make sure the model learns the right patterns.

2. **Forward Propagation:**
   Once the data is prepared, it is fed into the neural network for processing. During forward propagation, the input data is passed through the network's layers, with each layer performing computations and passing the output to the next layer. The last layer generates the model's prediction.

3. **Loss Computation:**
   After making a prediction, the model compares it to the correct answer and calculates the "loss," or error. The goal is to reduce this loss. For example, in classification tasks, the loss could measure how far the predicted category is from the actual one, while in regression tasks, it might measure how far off the predicted number is from the real value.

4. **Backpropagation**
   Backpropagation is a key algorithm used to update the model's parameters based on the calculated loss. In simple terms, it's a method for adjusting the model's settings to reduce the error (loss). It works by calculating how much each setting needs to change to make the model more

accurate, and then making those changes to reduce the error.

Optimisation is about fine-tuning the neural network's parameters during training, enhancing its performance to make better predictions. Some of the key optimisation techniques used in deep learning include:

1. **Gradient Descent**
   This is a common method for adjusting the model's settings to reduce error. It works by gradually making small changes to the settings, moving in the direction that leads to the smallest possible error. The process continues until the model's performance improves as much as possible.

2. **Learning Rate Scheduling**
   The learning rate controls how big each change to the model's settings is. If the learning rate is too high, the model might make too big a jump and miss the best solution. If it's too low, the process might take too long. Learning rate scheduling adjusts this rate during training to help the model learn more effectively.

3. **Regularisation**
   Sometimes, a model can become too focused on the training data, learning patterns that are too specific to that data. This is known as overfitting, where the model performs well on the training data but struggles to make accurate predictions on new, unseen data. Regularisation techniques add penalties during the training process to prevent overfitting, encouraging the model to learn more general patterns. This helps the model generalise better, meaning it can apply what it has learned to new data and make more accurate predictions in real-world situations.

4. **Momentum and Adaptive Methods**
   These techniques help speed up the training process. Momentum helps the model continue making improvements in the right direction, while adaptive methods like Adam and RMSprop adjust the learning rate during training to make the model's updates more effective.

In conclusion, training and optimisation are essential for developing effective deep learning models. By understanding how these processes work and using the right techniques, we can create models that are more accurate, faster, and better at handling real-world problems in various fields.

The Future of Deep Learning

As we stand on the cusp of a new era in artificial intelligence, the future of deep learning holds immense promise and potential for groundbreaking advancements. In this chapter, we will explore the trajectory of deep learning and its implications, while also delving into the ethical considerations that accompany its evolution.

Unsupervised Learning: One of the most intriguing frontiers in deep learning is unsupervised learning, where algorithms can extract meaningful patterns and structures from unlabelled data. This capability has the potential to unlock new insights and discoveries across various domains, from uncovering hidden correlations in complex datasets to enabling more efficient knowledge representation.

Reinforcement Learning: Another area of significant growth is reinforcement learning, where agents learn to make sequences of decisions through trial and error, aiming to maximise cumulative rewards. This paradigm has already demonstrated remarkable success in fields such as robotics, gaming, and autonomous systems, and its continued development could lead to more adaptive and intelligent machines.

Efficient Neural Network Architectures: The quest for more efficient and scalable neural network architectures is driving research into areas such as sparse neural networks, neural architecture search, and model compression. These endeavours seek to reduce the computational and memory requirements of deep learning models, making them more accessible and practical for a wider range of applications.

Ethical Considerations: As deep learning continues to permeate various aspects of society, ethical considerations become increasingly paramount. Issues such as algorithmic bias, privacy concerns, and the societal impact of AI-driven decision-making demand careful attention. Striking a balance between technological advancement and ethical responsibility will be crucial in shaping the future landscape of deep learning.

The Intersection of Deep Learning and Other Disciplines: The future of deep learning is intricately linked with interdisciplinary collaboration. The fusion of deep learning with fields such as neuroscience, cognitive science, and psychology holds the potential to not only enhance our understanding of intelligence but also inspire novel approaches to AI that are more aligned with human cognition.

In conclusion, the future of deep learning is poised to be a transformative force, driving innovation across industries and reshaping our relationship with technology. However, as we navigate this frontier, it is imperative to remain vigilant about the ethical implications and societal ramifications of our advancements. By embracing a holistic approach that integrates technological progress with ethical stewardship, we can harness the full potential of deep learning while ensuring that its benefits are realised in a responsible and equitable manner.

Chapter 12
ML vs DL vs DS vs AI

In this chapter, we will explore the differences between Machine Learning (ML), Deep Learning (DL), Data Science (DS), and Artificial Intelligence (AI) in a way that's accessible to everyone, regardless of their technical background. These terms are often used interchangeably, but they represent distinct concepts within the field of AI, and understanding their differences is crucial for grasping the broader landscape of artificial intelligence.

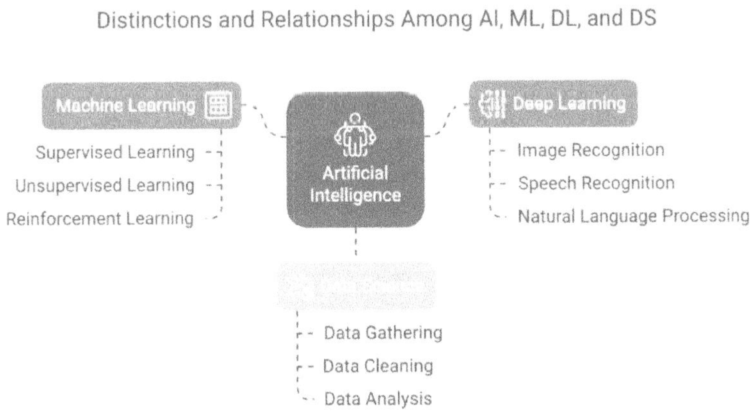

Machine Learning (ML) is like guiding a computer to understand and learn from examples. Imagine you have a friend who's learning to identify different types of fruits. You show them an apple and say, "This is an apple." Then you show them a banana and say, "This is a banana." After seeing many examples, your friend starts to recognise apples and bananas on their own. In the same way, ML algorithms learn from data to make predictions or decisions without being explicitly programmed to do so.

Deep Learning (DL) is a specialised form of ML that mimics the way the human brain works. It uses artificial neural networks with multiple layers to process data and identify patterns. For example, when you look at a photo of a cat, your brain processes the image in layers, recognising the edges, shapes, and finally the cat itself. DL does something similar with data, allowing computers to recognise complex patterns and make decisions based on them.

Data Science (DS) is like being a detective who solves mysteries using clues. In the world of data, these clues are pieces of information that can be found in numbers, words, images, and more. Data scientists use various tools and techniques to gather, clean, and analyse these clues to uncover valuable insights and solve real-world problems.

Artificial Intelligence (AI) is the big picture. It's like creating a robot that can think and act like a human. AI encompasses ML, DL, DS, and other technologies, aiming to build systems that can perform tasks that would typically require human intelligence, such as understanding language, recognising objects, making decisions, and even learning from experience.

Now, let's compare these concepts in more detail:

Machine Learning (ML): ML algorithms process data to recognise patterns and make predictions or decisions based on them. There are different types of ML, such as supervised learning (where the algorithm is trained on labelled data), unsupervised learning (where the algorithm finds patterns in unlabelled data), and reinforcement learning (where the algorithm learns by trial and error).

ML is used in various applications, including recommendation systems (like those used by streaming services to suggest movies), fraud detection, and predictive maintenance in manufacturing.

Deep Learning (DL): DL uses artificial neural networks with multiple layers to process data and identify patterns.

It's particularly good at tasks like image and speech recognition, natural language processing, and autonomous driving.

DL has led to breakthroughs in areas such as medical diagnosis, where it can analyse medical images and help doctors detect diseases more accurately.

Data Science (DS): DS involves gathering, cleaning, and analysing data to uncover valuable insights and solve real-world problems.

It uses techniques from fields like statistics, machine learning, and data visualisation to make sense of complex data sets.

DS is used in a wide range of applications, from predicting customer behaviour in e-commerce to optimising supply chains in logistics.

Artificial Intelligence (AI): AI aims to create systems that can perform tasks that would typically require human intelligence.

It encompasses ML, DL, DS, and other areas such as robotics, expert systems, and natural language processing.

AI is used in diverse fields, including healthcare (for diagnosing diseases and personalising treatment plans), finance (for fraud detection and risk assessment), and entertainment (for creating personalised recommendations and experiences).

In summary, ML focuses on teaching computers to learn from data, DL uses neural networks to process data and identify patterns, DS involves uncovering insights from data to solve real-world problems, and AI aims to create systems that can perform tasks that would typically require human intelligence.

Key Characteristics

Machine Learning (ML)

I. Learning from Data: ML systems leverage algorithms to recognise patterns and make decisions based on data inputs.

II. Task-Specific: ML is often task-specific, meaning it excels at particular tasks for which it has been trained.

III. Adaptability: ML models can adapt and improve as they encounter new data, enhancing their accuracy and effectiveness.

Deep Learning (DL)

I. Neural Networks: DL relies on deep neural networks, enabling it to automatically learn and represent features from data.

II. Complex Pattern Recognition: DL is particularly adept at tasks such as image and speech recognition, where intricate patterns need to be identified.

III. Hierarchical Learning: DL models learn hierarchical representations of data, allowing them to understand and process information at multiple levels of abstraction. This means that the model gradually breaks down complex data into simpler parts and then combines them to understand the bigger picture, like recognizing a face by first identifying its basic features, then its parts, and finally the whole face.

Data Science (DS)

I. Interdisciplinary: DS integrates concepts from statistics, mathematics, computer science, and domain-specific knowledge to extract insights from data.

II. Data Exploration: DS involves exploring and analysing data to uncover trends, patterns, and relationships.

III. Decision Support: The ultimate goal of DS is to provide actionable insights that can inform decision-making processes.

Artificial Intelligence (AI)

I. Reasoning and Problem Solving: AI systems are designed to reason, solve problems, and make decisions based on available information.

II. Learning and Adaptation: AI encompasses both rule-based systems and learning-based systems, allowing machines to adapt and improve. Rule-based systems follow fixed instructions to make decisions (like a recipe), while learning-based systems improve over time by learning from data (like how Netflix suggests shows based on what you've watched).

III. Natural Language Processing: Advanced AI systems can understand and generate human language, enabling effective communication between humans and machines.

Summarising the Distinctions

1. Relationship Between ML and AI: ML is a crucial component of AI. It empowers AI systems to learn from data, adapt, and improve their performance.

2. DL as a Subset of ML: While all deep learning is machine learning, not all machine learning is deep learning. Deep learning is a specialised field within ML that focuses on deep neural networks.

3. DS as the Foundation: Data Science serves as the foundation for both Machine Learning and Deep Learning. It involves data collection, cleaning, exploration, and analysis, providing the essential groundwork for these technologies.

4. AI - The Grand Vision: AI is the overarching vision that incorporates ML, DL, and DS, striving to create intelligent systems that can exhibit human-like cognitive functions.

Practical Applications and Real-World Impact

1. ML in Action: ML applications range from recommendation systems (like those on streaming platforms) to fraud detection in banking.

2. DL Transforming Industries: Deep Learning has transformed industries with applications in image and speech recognition, autonomous vehicles, and healthcare diagnostics.

3. DS Informing Decision-Making: Data Science is instrumental in business analytics, predictive modelling, and guiding strategic decisions across various sectors.

4. AI Shaping the Future: AI's grand vision is evident in virtual assistants, autonomous systems, and the potential for machines to exhibit general intelligence in the future.

In conclusion, machine learning, deep learning, data science, and artificial intelligence are distinct yet interconnected disciplines that play pivotal roles in shaping the future of technology. Understanding the differences and relationships between these concepts is essential for navigating the complex landscape of modern AI and leveraging their unique capabilities to drive innovation and progress. As we continue to explore and harness the potential of these disciplines, it is crucial to uphold ethical considerations and responsible practices to ensure that their benefits are maximised for the betterment of society as a whole.

Chapter 13
Natural Language Processing (NLP)

In the vast landscape of artificial intelligence, one of the most fascinating terrains to explore is Natural Language Processing, commonly known as NLP. This chapter delves into the intricacies of how machines comprehend and generate human language, bringing us closer to a future where meaningful communication between humans and machines is not just possible but seamless.

The Significance of NLP

Natural language is the primary means of communication between humans, and enabling machines to understand and process natural language has been a longstanding goal of AI research. NLP plays a crucial role in various applications, including language translation, sentiment analysis, chatbots, and information retrieval. By enabling machines to understand and generate human language, NLP has the potential to revolutionise how we interact with technology.

Unraveling the Tapestry of NLP

Understanding the Essence

Natural Language Processing (NLP) is not just about decoding words; it's about imbuing machines with the ability to comprehend and engage with human language on a profound level. At its essence, NLP seeks to unravel the intricate tapestry of communication by endowing machines with the capacity to understand the nuances, context, and subtleties embedded in our linguistic expressions.

Consider a scenario where a machine not only recognises the words you say but comprehends the underlying meaning, grasps the cultural connotations, and interprets the subtle nuances of language – that is the essence of NLP. It extends beyond the mere recognition of speech patterns; it involves deciphering the intricacies of human communication, such as humour, sarcasm, and idiomatic expressions.

NLP strives to merge the systematic and logical precision of machines with the intricate diversity and ever-evolving nuances of human language. It involves equipping machines with linguistic intelligence, enabling them not only to process information but to truly understand the essence of what is being conveyed. This intersection of artificial intelligence and linguistics marks a pivotal moment in our technological evolution, where machines move beyond scripted responses to engage in meaningful and contextually relevant conversations with humans. In essence, NLP is the key that unlocks the door to a future where communication between humans and machines transcends the mechanical and becomes profoundly human-like.

Historical Context

The roots of Natural Language Processing can be traced back to the early days of artificial intelligence, a time when pioneers in the field sought to imbue machines with the ability to understand and interpret human language. The quest for creating intelligent machines capable of meaningful communication has been a driving force since the inception of AI research.

In the 1950s and 1960s, early endeavours in language translation marked the nascent stages of NLP. Researchers, driven by the vision of breaking down language barriers, embarked on projects like Georgetown-IBM Automatic Translation (GAIT) and the development of the first-ever machine translation system. These early attempts laid the groundwork for what would later become a dynamic and rapidly evolving field.

As technology advanced, the focus shifted from simple translation to more intricate aspects of language understanding. The 1970s saw the emergence of rule-based systems, where explicit linguistic rules were programmed to facilitate language processing. Nonetheless, these systems found it difficult to handle the complexities and dynamic nuances of human language.

The 1980s witnessed a shift towards statistical approaches in NLP, driven by the availability of larger datasets and computational power. Researchers explored probabilistic models and machine learning techniques to improve language understanding. Despite notable progress, the field faced challenges in handling ambiguity and context, limiting the practical applications of NLP.

The late 20th century and early 21st century marked a turning point with the advent of computational linguistics, an interdisciplinary field that combines linguistics, computer science, and artificial intelligence to enable computers to process and understand human language. Researchers began incorporating linguistic theories into algorithms, allowing machines to analyse the structure and meaning of language. This period saw the integration of machine learning into Natural Language Processing (NLP), where models could learn from data to perform tasks such as translation and sentiment analysis. These advancements paved the way for more sophisticated models, setting the stage for the next era of NLP.

The breakthroughs of the 2010s, fuelled by the rise of deep learning and neural networks, propelled NLP into a new dimension. Models like Word2Vec, GloVe, and the transformer architecture revolutionised language representation and understanding. The introduction of pre-trained language models, such as BERT (Bidirectional Encoder Representations from Transformers) and GPT (Generative Pre-trained Transformer), marked a paradigm shift in NLP capabilities.

Today, NLP stands at the forefront of AI research, with continuous advancements pushing the boundaries of language understanding.

The historical journey of NLP reflects not only technological progress but also the persistent human endeavour to bridge the communication gap between man and machine. From early dreams of language translation to contemporary breakthroughs in deep learning, the historical context of NLP is a testament to the relentless pursuit of making machines truly conversant in the language of humanity.

The Building Blocks of NLP

Linguistics and AI

At the core of NLP lies a deep understanding of linguistics. Machines are trained to recognise syntax (the rules governing the structure of sentences), semantics (the meaning of words and sentences), and pragmatics (how context influences the interpretation of language), mirroring the way humans comprehend language. This intersection of linguistics and artificial intelligence is what propels NLP into the realm of true language understanding.

Tokenisation and Parsing

To make sense of sentences, NLP relies on tokenisation and parsing. Tokenisation breaks down text into individual words or phrases, while parsing determines the grammatical structure and relationships between these elements. These processes lay the foundation for machines to grasp the meaning encoded in human language.

NLP Applications in Everyday Life

NLP's diverse applications span industries, leveraging language understanding to drive innovation and efficiency. Its impact ranges from healthcare and customer service to finance and education. Here is a list of top applications showcasing the versatility and transformative potential of NLP.

Virtual Assistants

NLP continues to power the virtual assistants we interact with daily, such as Siri, Alexa, and Google Assistant. These intelligent systems have evolved to understand and respond to natural language queries, providing information, setting reminders, and even engaging in casual conversations. The integration of NLP has transformed these devices into intuitive companions, enhancing user experience and productivity.

Sentiment Analysis

Businesses are increasingly leveraging NLP for sentiment analysis to gauge public opinion on products or services. By analysing social media posts, customer reviews, and feedback, NLP algorithms can discern sentiments, identifying trends and patterns in user sentiment. This valuable insight helps companies make data-driven decisions to enhance user experience, improve products, and tailor marketing strategies to better meet customer needs.

Language Translation

The dream of a universal translator is rapidly becoming a reality with the advancements in NLP. Platforms like Google Translate and other language translation services utilise advanced NLP algorithms to break down language barriers, facilitating seamless communication across the globe. These systems not only translate words but also aim to capture the nuances of language, enabling more accurate and natural-sounding translations. As NLP technology continues to advance, the potential for improved cross-lingual communication and understanding is vast.

Text Generation and Summarisation

NLP has made significant strides in text generation and summarisation, enabling machines to generate coherent and contextually relevant text. From chatbots that engage in natural conversations to automated content generation for news articles and reports, NLP-powered systems are increasingly capable of producing human-like text. Additionally, NLP algorithms can summarise lengthy documents, extracting key information and presenting it in a concise and digestible format, saving time and effort for users.

Conversational AI

Conversational AI, powered by NLP, is revolutionising customer service and support. Chatbots and virtual agents equipped with NLP capabilities can engage in natural, context-aware conversations with users, providing personalised assistance, answering queries, and even handling transactions. This technology is reshaping the way businesses interact with customers, offering efficient and responsive support around the clock.

Legal and Compliance

In the legal and compliance sector, NLP is employed to analyse and review large volumes of legal documents, contracts, and regulatory filings. NLP algorithms can extract key information, identify relevant clauses, and categorise documents, streamlining the process of legal research, due diligence, and compliance management.

Education and E-Learning

NLP is increasingly being integrated into educational technology and e-learning platforms. NLP-powered systems can provide personalised learning experiences, assess student performance through automated grading and feedback, and facilitate language learning through interactive exercises and language proficiency assessment.

Content Recommendation and Personalisation

NLP plays a crucial role in content recommendation systems used by streaming platforms, news websites, and e-commerce platforms. By analysing user preferences, behaviour, and feedback, NLP algorithms can recommend personalised content, products, and services, enhancing user engagement and satisfaction.

Healthcare Informatics

In addition to analysing medical records, NLP is utilised in healthcare informatics for tasks such as extracting information from clinical notes, standardising medical terminology, and identifying adverse drug reactions. NLP-powered systems contribute to improving patient care, clinical decision-making, and medical research.

Social Media Monitoring and Analysis

NLP is employed to monitor and analyse social media conversations, trends, and public sentiment. Brands and organisations use NLP to gain insights into consumer opinions, brand perception, and emerging trends, informing their marketing strategies and communication efforts.

Voice of Customer Analysis

NLP is utilised for voice of customer analysis, where customer feedback from various sources such as surveys, reviews, and call transcripts is analysed to understand customer preferences, concerns, and satisfaction levels. NLP enables businesses to derive actionable insights from unstructured customer feedback data.

Cross-Domain Information Integration

NLP facilitates the integration of information from diverse sources and formats, enabling the extraction and synthesis of knowledge from unstructured data. This capability is valuable in fields such as knowledge management, data integration, and information retrieval across different domains.

As NLP technology continues to advance, its applications are expected to expand further, driving innovation and transformation across industries and domains. The ability of NLP to process and understand human language is unlocking new possibilities for how we interact with technology, make decisions, and access information in the digital age.

Technologies Behind NLP

NLP relies on a combination of linguistic, statistical, and machine learning techniques to process and understand natural language. Key technologies used in NLP include tokenisation (breaking text into smaller units like words or phrases), part-of-speech tagging (identifying grammatical categories like nouns and verbs for each word), named entity recognition (extracting names of people, places, or dates from text), syntactic parsing (analysing the grammatical structure of sentences), and semantic analysis (understanding the meaning of words and phrases based on context). Additionally, machine learning models such as recurrent neural networks (RNNs) and transformer-based architectures like BERT and GPT-3 have significantly advanced the capabilities of NLP systems.

NLP Challenges and Breakthroughs

Ambiguity and Context

One of the significant challenges in NLP is handling ambiguity and understanding context. Human language is rife with nuances, double entendres, and cultural references, making it a complex puzzle for machines to solve. Ongoing research focuses on improving contextual understanding, pushing the boundaries of NLP capabilities.

Breakthroughs in Neural Networks

The rise of deep learning and neural networks has propelled NLP to new heights. Models like BERT (Bidirectional Encoder Representations from Transformers) and GPT (Generative Pre-trained Transformer) showcase the power of large-scale language models, enabling machines to generate coherent and contextually relevant text.

The Ethical Dimensions of NLP

Bias and Fairness

As NLP systems learn from vast datasets, they inherit the biases present in that data. This draws attention to ethical questions regarding fairness and inclusivity. Researchers and developers grapple with the challenge of creating NLP models that are unbiased and reflect the diversity of human experiences.

Privacy and Security

The ability of NLP systems to analyse and process textual data poses privacy and security concerns. Striking a balance between extracting valuable insights and respecting user privacy is an ongoing challenge in the ethical deployment of NLP technologies.

Future Frontiers of NLP

Conversational AI

The future of NLP holds the promise of more natural and engaging conversations with machines. Advancements in conversational AI aim to make interactions with virtual assistants and chatbots indistinguishable from human-to-human conversations.

Multimodal NLP

As technology advances, the integration of NLP with other modalities, such as images and videos, becomes increasingly relevant. Multimodal NLP seeks to enhance language understanding by incorporating visual and auditory cues, opening up new possibilities for human-machine interaction.

NLP in the Layman's Perspective

Bridging the Gap

In a world inundated with technology, understanding the basics of NLP becomes essential for the layman. This chapter aims to demystify the complexities, making the fascinating realm of NLP accessible and relatable to everyone.

Everyday Applications

From the smartphone in your pocket to the smart speakers in your home, NLP is woven into the fabric of everyday life. Recognising its presence and understanding its functionalities empower individuals to make informed decisions about the technology they interact with.

Case Study: NLP in Biotech and Healthcare

To illustrate the practical impact of NLP, let's consider the example of a biotech and healthcare company that leverages NLP to analyse medical literature and clinical notes. By using NLP to extract relevant information from a vast amount of unstructured text, the company can identify potential drug interactions, adverse effects, and new treatment options. This not only accelerates the process of drug discovery and development but also contributes to improved patient care and outcomes.

Conclusion

Natural Language Processing is a pivotal area of AI that holds immense potential for transforming how we interact with technology and how businesses operate. By enabling machines to understand and process human language, NLP opens up new possibilities for innovation across various domains. However, it is essential to address the challenges and ethical considerations associated with NLP to ensure its responsible and beneficial use. As NLP continues to evolve, it will undoubtedly play a central role in shaping the future of artificial intelligence and its applications in our daily lives.

Chapter 14
Speech Recognition

Speech recognition, also known as automatic speech recognition (ASR) or speech-to-text, is a technology that enables machines to understand and interpret human speech. In simpler terms, it allows computers to listen to spoken words and convert them into written text. This technology has become increasingly common in our daily lives, powering virtual assistants like Siri, Alexa, and Google Assistant, as well as speech-to-text transcription services.

When a person speaks into a device, such as a smartphone or a smart speaker, the audio input is processed by the speech recognition system. The system then works to identify individual words and phrases, understand the context in which they are used, and accurately convert them into written text. This process requires the system to recognise the words being spoken and understand the nuances of human speech, such as accents, intonation, and variations in pronunciation.

In essence, speech recognition allows us to communicate with computers and devices using our voice, making it easier to perform tasks, ask questions, and interact with technology in a more natural and intuitive way.

The history of speech recognition dates back to the 1950s when researchers began exploring the possibility of creating machines that could understand and process human speech. Over the years, significant advancements in machine learning, neural networks, and natural language processing have propelled speech recognition to new heights, making it an integral part of our daily lives.

One of the key breakthroughs in speech recognition came with the development of deep learning algorithms and neural networks. These technologies have significantly improved the accuracy and reliability of speech recognition systems, enabling them to understand and transcribe spoken language with remarkable precision.

The intricacies of speech recognition lie in its ability to process and interpret spoken language. It involves the use of advanced algorithms and machine learning models to analyse audio input, identify individual words and phrases, and convert them into text. This process requires the system to understand not only the words being spoken but also the context, tone, and nuances of human speech.

Features of Speech Recognition Systems

Speech recognition systems have several key features that enable them to accurately interpret and transcribe spoken language. Some of the prominent features of speech recognition systems include:

1. **Audio Input Processing**: Speech recognition systems are designed to process audio input from various sources, such as microphones, telephones, or audio recordings. They analyse the incoming audio signals to identify speech patterns and distinguish them from background noise.

2. **Language Modelling**: These systems utilise language models to understand the structure and patterns of natural language. This includes recognising grammar, syntax, and vocabulary to interpret spoken words and phrases in context.

3. **Acoustic Modelling**: Acoustic modelling is a crucial feature that helps the system understand the sound patterns of spoken language. It involves analysing the acoustic properties of speech, such as phonemes and their variations, to accurately recognise and differentiate between different spoken sounds.

4. **Speaker Adaptation**: Some advanced speech recognition systems incorporate speaker adaptation features, allowing them to adapt to the specific speech patterns and accents of

individual users. This can improve accuracy and recognition for diverse user populations.

5. **Contextual Understanding**: Modern speech recognition systems aim to understand the context in which words and phrases are spoken. This involves considering the surrounding words, the topic of conversation, and the user's intent to provide more accurate transcriptions and responses.

6. **Real-Time Processing**: Many speech recognition systems are capable of processing and transcribing speech in real time, enabling immediate feedback and interaction with users. This feature is particularly important for applications such as virtual assistants and live transcription services.

7. **Noise Cancellation**: To improve accuracy, speech recognition systems often incorporate noise cancellation algorithms to filter out background noise and focus on the speech signal, especially in noisy environments.

8. **Multilingual Support**: Advanced speech recognition systems are designed to support multiple languages, allowing users to interact with the system in their preferred language and enabling cross-lingual applications.

9. **Integration with Natural Language Processing (NLP)**: Speech recognition systems often integrate with NLP technologies to further understand and process the transcribed text, enabling tasks such as language translation, sentiment analysis, and information retrieval.

These features collectively enable speech recognition systems to accurately interpret and transcribe spoken language, making them valuable tools for a wide range of applications, from virtual assistants and dictation software to customer service and accessibility services.

Stepwise Breakdown of Speech Recognition

Speech recognition works through a series of complex processes that involve analysing and interpreting spoken language. Here's a simplified overview of how speech recognition works:

1. **Audio Input**: The process begins with the capture of audio input, typically through a microphone or other recording device. The audio signal containing the spoken words is then digitised and processed for analysis.

2. **Preprocessing**: The incoming audio signal undergoes preprocessing, which involves tasks such as noise reduction, normalisation, and segmentation to isolate the speech signal from background noise and other audio artefacts.

3. **Feature Extraction**: The preprocessed audio signal is then analysed to extract relevant features that represent the characteristics of the speech signal. This may involve identifying key elements such as phonemes, spectral features, and other acoustic properties of speech.

4. **Acoustic Modelling**: The extracted features are used to create acoustic models that represent the relationship between spoken sounds and their corresponding linguistic units, such as phonemes, words, or phrases. This step is crucial for the system to recognise and differentiate between different spoken sounds.

5. **Language Modelling**: Concurrently, language models are employed to understand the structure and patterns of natural language. This involves recognising grammar, syntax, and vocabulary to interpret spoken words and phrases in context.

6. **Decoding and Matching**: The acoustic and language models are used in combination to decode the speech signal and match it to the most probable sequence of words or phrases.

This process involves statistical analysis and pattern matching to determine the most likely transcription of the spoken input.

7. **Post-Processing and Interpretation**: Once the speech signal has been transcribed into text, post-processing techniques may be applied to refine the transcription and improve accuracy. This may involve contextual analysis, error correction, and language-specific rules to enhance the quality of the transcribed text.

8. **Output**: The final output of the speech recognition process is the transcribed text, which represents the spoken words in written form. This text can then be used for various applications, such as voice commands for virtual assistants, speech-to-text transcription, or input for natural language processing systems.

Modern speech recognition systems often incorporate advanced machine learning algorithms, neural networks, and deep learning techniques to improve accuracy and adapt to diverse speech patterns and languages. Additionally, ongoing research and development in the field continue to drive advancements in speech recognition technology.

Speech Recognition Algorithms

Speech recognition algorithms are the computational methods and techniques used to process and interpret spoken language. These algorithms play a crucial role in converting audio input into written text and are essential components of speech recognition systems. Here are some of the different types of speech recognition algorithms commonly used in the field:

1. **Hidden Markov Models (HMMs)**: HMMs have been a foundational algorithm in speech recognition. They model the statistical properties of speech signals and are used to represent the temporal sequence of speech sounds, meaning they capture the order and timing of spoken sounds, which is crucial for understanding language. HMMs are particularly effective in modelling the dynamics of speech, allowing systems to track how sounds change over time. This capability has made them widely used in acoustic modelling for speech recognition, where they help create mathematical models that link audio signals to corresponding linguistic units, such as phonemes or words, enabling accurate interpretation of spoken language.

2. **Gaussian Mixture Models (GMMs)**: GMMs are often used alongside HMMs for acoustic modelling in speech recognition. They model the probability distribution of acoustic features, such as the spectral characteristics of speech, which refer to the different frequencies present in a speech signal and how they vary over time. These features are key to distinguishing different speech sounds. GMMs are instrumental in capturing the variability of speech sounds, accounting for differences in pronunciation, tone, and background noise, thereby improving the system's ability to accurately recognise and interpret spoken language.

3. **Deep Neural Networks (DNNs)**: Deep learning techniques, particularly deep neural networks, have revolutionised speech recognition. DNNs are used for acoustic modelling and have shown significant improvements in speech recognition accuracy. They are capable of learning complex hierarchical representations of speech features and have become a cornerstone of modern speech recognition systems.

4. **Convolutional Neural Networks (CNNs)**: CNNs, known for their effectiveness in image recognition, have also been applied to speech recognition tasks. They are used to process spectrogram representations of speech signals and have

shown promise in capturing local dependencies in speech features.

5. **Recurrent Neural Networks (RNNs)**: Recurrent Neural Networks (RNNs), including variants like Long Short-Term Memory (LSTM) and Gated Recurrent Unit (GRU), are well-suited for modelling sequential data, making them valuable for speech recognition. They can capture temporal dependencies in speech signals, meaning they understand how earlier parts of a speech sequence influence later parts. This is crucial for recognising the flow and structure of spoken language. RNNs are used for acoustic modelling, which involves interpreting speech sounds, and for language modelling, which helps the system predict what words are most likely to appear next in a sentence. For example, if someone says 'I am going to the', the system can predict that 'store' or 'market' is more likely to come next than something random like 'elephant'. This helps the speech recognition system make more accurate guesses about what people are saying, even if there's background noise or if the speaker's voice isn't perfectly clear.

6. **Connectionist Temporal Classification (CTC)**: CTC is a technique used in conjunction with neural networks for sequence modelling and alignment in speech recognition. It allows the neural network to directly output sequences of characters or phonemes without requiring explicit alignment between the input and output sequences.

7. **Attention Mechanisms**: Attention mechanisms, often used in conjunction with neural networks, enable the model to focus on relevant parts of the input sequence when making predictions. They have been applied to improve the performance of speech recognition systems, particularly in handling long input sequences.

8. **End-to-End Models**: End-to-end speech recognition models aim to directly map input speech signals to transcribed text

without the need for intermediate representations or separate components for acoustic and language modelling. These models often leverage deep learning architectures and have shown promise in simplifying the speech recognition pipeline.

These algorithms, often used in combination, form the backbone of modern speech recognition systems. They enable the accurate processing, interpretation, and transcription of spoken language, and ongoing research continues to advance the capabilities of speech recognition algorithms.

Applications of Speech Recognition

Speech recognition technology has a wide range of applications across various industries and domains. Here are some of the key applications of speech recognition:

1. **Virtual Assistants**: Virtual assistants, such as Siri, Alexa, Google Assistant, and Cortana, utilise speech recognition to understand and respond to spoken commands. Users can interact with these virtual assistants using natural language, enabling tasks such as setting reminders, checking the weather, playing music, and controlling smart home devices.

2. **Transcription Services**: Speech recognition technology is used for speech-to-text transcription services, allowing users to dictate spoken language and have it accurately transcribed into written text. This is particularly useful for professionals in fields such as healthcare, legal, and journalism, as well as for creating captions for videos and live events.

3. **Customer Service and Call Centres**: Speech recognition is employed in customer service applications to automate call routing, transcribe customer inquiries, and provide interactive voice response (IVR) systems. This technology streamlines

customer interactions and can improve the efficiency of call centre operations.

4. **Accessibility Services**: Speech recognition plays a crucial role in accessibility services for individuals with disabilities. It enables hands-free interaction with devices, facilitates communication for individuals with speech impairments, and supports the development of assistive technologies for people with visual or motor disabilities.

5. **Healthcare Documentation**: In the healthcare industry, speech recognition technology is used for medical transcription, allowing healthcare professionals to dictate patient notes, medical reports, and documentation, which are then transcribed into electronic health records (EHRs) and other medical documents.

6. **Language Translation**: Speech recognition technology is integrated into language translation applications, enabling real-time translation of spoken language into different languages. This has significant implications for cross-lingual communication and international business interactions.

7. **Automotive Systems**: Speech recognition is utilised in automotive systems for hands-free operation of in-vehicle infotainment systems, navigation, and voice-activated controls. This enhances driver safety and convenience by minimising distractions while driving.

8. **Dictation and Voice Commands**: Speech recognition technology is used for dictation software, allowing users to dictate text for word processing, email composition, and note-taking. Additionally, voice commands are employed in various applications, including smart home devices, mobile phones, and wearable technology.

9. **Security and Authentication**: Speech recognition can be used for biometric authentication and voice-based security

systems. It enables voice authentication for access control, secure voice-based transactions, and identity verification.

10. **Education and Language Learning**: Speech recognition technology can be integrated into educational applications to provide language learning support, pronunciation feedback, and interactive language exercises for students and language learners.

These applications demonstrate the versatility and impact of speech recognition technology across diverse domains, and ongoing advancements in artificial intelligence and natural language processing continue to expand its potential applications.

Advantages of Speech Recognition

Here's how speech recognition technology has revolutionised the way we interact with devices.

1. Hands-Free Operation: Speech recognition enables hands-free interaction with devices, allowing users to perform tasks and access information without the need for manual input.

2. Accessibility: It provides accessibility for individuals with physical disabilities or those who have difficulty using traditional input methods.

3. Increased Productivity: Speech recognition can enhance productivity by enabling faster data entry, dictation, and command execution.

4. Multimodal Interaction: It complements other input methods, such as touch and keyboard, to offer a multimodal interaction experience.

5. Natural User Interface: Speech recognition offers a natural and intuitive way to interact with technology, especially in applications like virtual assistants and smart home devices.

Disadvantages of Speech Recognition

Despite its many advantages, speech recognition technology also presents some notable disadvantages worth considering.

1. Accuracy Challenges: Speech recognition systems may struggle with accurately interpreting diverse accents, dialects, and variations in speech patterns.

2. Privacy Concerns: Storing and processing voice data raises privacy and security concerns, especially in the context of data breaches and unauthorised access.

3. Environmental Factors: Background noise, poor audio quality, and non-ideal recording environments can impact the accuracy of speech recognition.

4. Learning Curve: Users may need time to adapt to speech recognition systems, and the technology may require training to improve accuracy.

5. Limited Vocabulary and Context Understanding: Speech recognition systems may face challenges in understanding context and handling specialised vocabulary or language models.

Challenges of Speech Recognition

Speech recognition technology faces several challenges, despite its significant advancements. Some of the key challenges include:

1. Accents and Dialects: Variations in accents and dialects pose a challenge for speech recognition systems. Different regional accents and pronunciation patterns can make it difficult for the system to accurately interpret and transcribe spoken language.

2. Background Noise: Ambient noise in the environment, such as chatter, music, or other sounds, can interfere with the accuracy of speech recognition. Filtering out background noise while accurately capturing the intended speech remains a significant challenge.

3. Contextual Understanding: Understanding the context in which words and phrases are used is crucial for accurate speech recognition. Ambiguities in language and the need to interpret meaning based on the surrounding words and phrases present a challenge for speech recognition systems.

4. Speaker Variability: Speech recognition systems must be able to adapt to variations in individual voices, including differences in pitch, tone, and speech patterns. Speaker variability adds complexity to the task of accurately transcribing speech.

5. Vocabulary and Language Models: The ability to recognise and interpret a wide vocabulary and diverse language models presents a challenge for speech recognition systems. Handling specialised terminology, slang, and rapidly evolving language usage requires robust language models.

6. Real-time Processing: Achieving real-time processing of spoken language with high accuracy is a technical challenge. Systems must be able to process and transcribe speech rapidly while maintaining precision and minimising latency.

7. Privacy and Security: Ensuring the privacy and security of sensitive voice data is a critical challenge. Speech recognition systems must address concerns related to data privacy, secure

storage of voice recordings, and protection against unauthorised access.

8. Adverse Conditions: Speech recognition performance can be affected by adverse conditions such as poor audio quality, low bandwidth, or non-ideal recording environments. Overcoming these adverse conditions to maintain accuracy is a challenge.

9. Emotional and Expressive Speech: Interpreting emotional or expressive speech, including variations in tone, emphasis, and non-verbal cues, presents a challenge for speech recognition systems, particularly in applications where understanding the speaker's emotional state is important.

10. Multilingual Support: Supporting multiple languages and dialects with high accuracy and consistency is a complex challenge for speech recognition systems, especially in multilingual and multicultural environments.

Addressing these challenges requires ongoing research and development in the fields of artificial intelligence, machine learning, natural language processing, and audio signal processing. As technology continues to advance, overcoming these challenges will be crucial for further improving the capabilities of speech recognition systems.

Chapter 15
AI Chatbots

In the realm of artificial intelligence, chatbots stand as a transformative technology that has revolutionised the way businesses and individuals interact with technology. These intelligent virtual assistants are designed to simulate human conversation and provide automated responses to user enquiries, enabling seamless and efficient communication across a wide range of applications. In this chapter, we will delve into the intricacies of AI chatbots, explore their fundamental principles, and shed light on their profound impact on the future of AI and human-computer interaction.

The Transformative Power of AI Chatbots in Modern Technology

Defining Chatbots

Chatbots are digital programmes designed to replicate human conversation, primarily through text or speech. Powered by Artificial Intelligence, these digital entities are capable of understanding user queries, interpreting intent, and providing relevant responses.

Understanding AI Chatbots

AI chatbots, also known as conversational agents or virtual assistants, are software applications that are programmed to conduct conversations with users through text or speech interfaces. These intelligent systems leverage natural language processing (NLP), machine learning, and other AI techniques to understand user queries, interpret their intent, and provide relevant and contextually appropriate responses. AI chatbots can be deployed across various platforms, including websites, messaging applications, and voice-enabled devices, offering users a convenient and efficient way to access information, perform tasks, and engage with businesses and services.

The Rise of Conversational AI

1. **Early Conversational Agents**
   The concept of conversational agents dates back to the 1960s, with early experiments like ELIZA, designed to engage in simple natural language conversations.

2. **Advancements in NLP**
   The advancement of Natural Language Processing (NLP) in recent decades has been pivotal in enhancing the capabilities of Chatbots. NLP enables these digital entities to comprehend and respond to human language in a more sophisticated manner.

3. **Integration with Messaging Platforms**
   The integration of Chatbots into popular messaging platforms, such as Facebook Messenger, WhatsApp, and Slack, has contributed to their widespread adoption and accessibility.

Fundamental Principles of AI Chatbots

AI chatbots rely on a combination of technologies and methodologies to deliver intelligent and contextually relevant interactions with users. Some of the key principles that underpin the functionality of AI chatbots include:

1. **Natural Language Processing (NLP):** NLP enables chatbots to understand and interpret human language, allowing them to analyse user queries, extract meaning, and generate appropriate responses. NLP techniques include tasks like text parsing, which breaks down sentences into smaller parts to understand their structure; sentiment analysis, which helps the chatbot detect whether the user is happy, angry, or

neutral; entity recognition, where the chatbot identifies important information like names or places; and language generation, which allows the chatbot to create clear and relevant responses based on the conversation. Together, these techniques enable chatbots to engage in meaningful and natural conversations with users.

2. **Machine Learning:** Machine learning algorithms empower chatbots to continuously improve their performance by learning from user interactions and feedback. Through the use of supervised and unsupervised learning techniques, chatbots can adapt to user preferences, refine their language models, and enhance their ability to understand and respond to a diverse range of queries.

3. **Contextual Understanding:** AI chatbots are designed to maintain context across conversations, enabling them to remember previous interactions, anticipate user needs, and provide personalised and relevant responses. Contextual understanding allows chatbots to engage in natural and coherent conversations, enhancing the user experience and fostering effective communication.

How Chatbots Work

1. **User Input Analysis**
   Chatbots begin by analysing user input, whether it's a text message, voice command, or any other form of communication.

2. **Intent Recognition**
   The system identifies the user's intent, determining what action or information the user is seeking.

3. **Context Understanding**
   Chatbots leverage context understanding to maintain

continuity in conversations, remembering previous interactions and user preferences.

4. **Response Generation**
   Based on the analysed input and recognised intent, the Chatbot generates a response, aiming to provide relevant and helpful information.

Applications of AI Chatbots

AI chatbots have permeated various industries and domains, transforming the way businesses and individuals engage with technology and access services. Some of the key applications of AI chatbots include:

1. **Customer Service**: Chatbots are widely used in customer service applications to provide instant support, answer frequently asked questions, and assist users with product information, troubleshooting, and enquiries. By automating routine interactions, chatbots enhance the efficiency of customer support operations and improve the overall customer experience.

2. **E-Commerce and Retail**: Chatbots are deployed in e-commerce and retail environments to assist customers with product recommendations, order tracking, and personalised shopping experiences. Chatbots can engage users in conversational commerce, guiding them through the purchase process and offering tailored assistance based on their preferences and browsing history.

3. **Healthcare and Wellness**: Chatbots are utilised in healthcare and wellness applications to provide medical advice, symptom assessment, medication reminders, and mental health support. Healthcare chatbots can offer personalised

recommendations, deliver health-related information, and facilitate remote consultations, improving access to healthcare services and promoting wellness.

4. **Financial Services**: Chatbots are integrated into financial services to provide account information, transaction support, financial advice, and personalised banking experiences. Financial chatbots can assist users with account management, budgeting, and investment guidance, offering convenient and secure interactions for banking customers.

Challenges and Future Directions

While AI chatbots have made significant strides in enhancing user engagement and automating interactions, they still face several challenges, such as understanding complex queries, maintaining conversational coherence, and addressing user privacy and data security concerns. Additionally, the ethical considerations surrounding the use of chatbots, such as transparency, accountability, and bias, require careful attention and responsible practices.

Looking ahead, the future of AI chatbots holds immense promise, with ongoing research and development focusing on advancing the capabilities of conversational agents, improving their language understanding, and enabling them to facilitate more intuitive and contextually meaningful conversations. As chatbot technology continues to evolve, it has the potential to further enhance customer engagement, streamline business operations, and foster seamless and efficient communication across diverse industries and applications.

In conclusion, AI chatbots stand as a cornerstone of artificial intelligence, empowering businesses and individuals to engage in natural and intelligent conversations with technology. Their applications span a wide spectrum of industries, from customer service and e-commerce to healthcare and financial services, enriching the way we interact with technology and access services.

As chatbot technology continues to advance, it is essential to uphold ethical considerations and responsible practices to ensure that its benefits are maximised for the betterment of society and the advancement of human-computer interaction.

Chapter 16
Computer Vision

In the realm of artificial intelligence, computer vision stands as a transformative technology that enables machines to interpret and understand the visual world. This remarkable field has revolutionised the way we perceive and interact with technology, empowering machines to analyse and derive meaningful insights from visual data. In this chapter, we will delve into the intricacies of computer vision, explore its fundamental principles, and shed light on its profound impact on the future of AI and human-computer interaction.

Harnessing the Power of Computer Vision within AI

Defining Computer Vision

Computer Vision is a branch of Artificial Intelligence that enables machines to analyse, comprehend, and make decisions from visual data. It seeks to replicate the human ability to process and comprehend information from images or videos, extending the realm of AI into the visual domain.

Understanding Computer Vision

Computer vision is a multidisciplinary field that focuses on enabling machines to gain high-level understanding from digital images or videos. It encompasses a wide range of techniques and methodologies aimed at extracting, analysing, and interpreting visual information to enable automated decision-making. By leveraging advanced algorithms, machine learning, and deep learning models, computer vision systems can recognise patterns, objects, and spatial relationships—such as the relative positions, sizes, and orientations of objects—within visual data, enabling them to perform tasks that mimic human visual perception.

The Journey from Pixels to Understanding

1. **Early Image Processing**
   The roots of computer vision trace back to the 1960s, with initial attempts focusing on basic image processing tasks like pattern recognition and edge detection, the latter of which identifies boundaries of objects in an image by detecting changes in brightness or contrast.

2. **Advancements in Algorithms**
   Over the decades, advancements in algorithms, particularly with the rise of machine learning, have propelled computer vision into a sophisticated discipline capable of complex visual tasks.

3. **Integration with Deep Learning**
   The synergy between computer vision and deep learning, particularly convolutional neural networks (CNNs), has revolutionised the field, enabling machines to learn hierarchical representations of visual data—where simple features like edges are detected in the initial layers, and more complex features, such as shapes or objects, are recognised in deeper layers.

Key Components of Computer Vision

1. **Image Acquisition**: The process of capturing visual data from various sources, such as cameras, sensors, or digital images, forms the foundation of computer vision. Image acquisition involves techniques for capturing high-quality visual data and ensuring its suitability for subsequent analysis and processing.

2. **Preprocessing and Feature Extraction**: Once visual data is acquired, preprocessing techniques are applied to enhance image quality, remove noise, and standardise the data for analysis. Feature extraction methods are then employed to identify relevant patterns, edges, textures, and shapes within the visual data, enabling the system to extract meaningful information for further analysis.

3. **Object Detection and Recognition**: Computer vision systems utilise object detection and recognition algorithms to identify and classify objects within visual data. These algorithms enable machines to detect and localise objects of interest, such as faces, vehicles, or specific items, within images or videos, facilitating tasks such as image segmentation, object tracking, and scene understanding.

4. **Image Understanding and Interpretation**: Advanced computer vision models are capable of understanding and interpreting the content of visual data, enabling them to derive semantic meaning (the deeper significance or context of objects in an image), context, and actionable insights from images or videos. This capability allows computer vision systems to perform tasks such as image classification, scene understanding, and content-based image retrieval.

A Quick Snapshot of How Computer Vision Works

1. **Image Acquisition**
   The process begins with acquiring visual data, whether in the form of images or video frames, through cameras or other sensors.

2. **Preprocessing**
   Preprocessing involves enhancing and cleaning the acquired data, addressing issues such as noise, lighting variations, or

distortions.

3. **Feature Extraction**
Computer vision algorithms extract features from the visual data, identifying patterns, shapes, and other relevant information.

4. **Recognition and Interpretation**
The system then recognises and interprets the visual content, making sense of objects, scenes, or even actions depicted in the images or videos.

Applications of Computer Vision

Computer vision has permeated various industries and domains, transforming the way businesses and individuals leverage visual data and interact with technology. Some of the major applications of computer vision include:

1. **Autonomous Vehicles**: Computer vision plays a pivotal role in enabling autonomous vehicles to perceive and interpret their surroundings, identify obstacles, and make real-time decisions based on visual data. By leveraging computer vision algorithms, autonomous vehicles can navigate complex environments, detect traffic signs, and ensure safe and efficient transportation.

2. **Healthcare and Medical Imaging**: Computer vision is utilised in healthcare for medical imaging analysis, disease diagnosis, and treatment planning. It enables the automated analysis of medical images, such as X-rays, MRIs, and CT scans, facilitating the detection of anomalies, tumours, and other medical conditions.

3. **Retail and E-Commerce**: Computer vision is employed in retail and e-commerce for visual search, product recognition,

and augmented reality applications. It enables users to search for products using images, receive personalised recommendations, and visualise products in real-world environments through augmented reality experiences.

4. **Industrial Automation and Quality Control**: Computer vision is integrated into industrial automation systems for quality control, defect detection, and process monitoring. It enables machines to inspect and analyse visual data from manufacturing processes, ensuring product quality, identifying defects, and optimising production efficiency.

Challenges and Considerations

1. **Robustness to Variations**
   Computer vision systems must be robust to variations in lighting, perspective, and occlusions, ensuring accurate recognition in diverse conditions.

2. **Ethical Implications**
   The use of computer vision in surveillance and facial recognition raises ethical considerations related to privacy, consent, and potential misuse.

3. **Data Bias and Fairness**
   Ensuring fairness in computer vision models and addressing biases in training data is a critical consideration to avoid perpetuating inequalities.

4. **Interpretable AI**
   The interpretability of computer vision models is essential, especially in applications with significant impact, such as healthcare and autonomous vehicles.

Future Directions

1. **Enhanced AR and VR Experiences**
   Computer vision is poised to elevate Augmented Reality (AR) and Virtual Reality (VR) experiences, providing more realistic and interactive virtual environments.

2. **Human-Robot Collaboration**
   As robots become more integrated into human spaces, computer vision facilitates seamless collaboration by allowing machines to understand and respond to human gestures and actions.

3. **Environmental Monitoring**
   Computer vision contributes to environmental monitoring by analysing satellite imagery, identifying deforestation, tracking wildlife, and assessing climate patterns.

4. **Assistive Technologies**
   In the realm of assistive technologies, computer vision aids individuals with visual impairments by providing real-time object recognition and scene descriptions.

In conclusion, computer vision plays a pivotal role in artificial intelligence, allowing machines to interpret and make sense of visual information. Its applications span a wide spectrum of industries, from autonomous vehicles and healthcare to retail and industrial automation, enriching the way we interact with technology and leverage visual data. As computer vision technology continues to advance, it is essential to uphold ethical considerations and responsible practices to ensure that its benefits are maximised for the betterment of society and the advancement of human-computer interaction.

Chapter 17
Practical AI
Applications in Energy, Finance, and Education

In the evolving landscape of Artificial Intelligence, this chapter delves into three distinct applications, each marking a milestone in the transformative journey of AI across diverse sectors. We will unravel the intricacies of Smart Grids in the Energy Industry, Algorithmic Trading in Finance, and Personalised Learning Platforms in Education. These applications showcase the convergence of advanced algorithms, real-time data analytics, and machine learning to redefine the boundaries of efficiency, decision-making, and individualised experiences. As we navigate through these AI-driven realms, we explore the impact, challenges, and potential of each application, offering insights into the profound changes they bring to their respective industries. Join this exploration of the intelligent intersections between technology and sectors crucial to our daily lives.

I. Smart Grids in the Energy Industry

The energy industry is undergoing a remarkable transformation with the integration of Artificial Intelligence, and one groundbreaking application leading the charge is the implementation of Smart Grids. In this chapter, we delve into the world of Smart Grids, where traditional power infrastructure meets the prowess of AI. These intelligent grids leverage real-time data, analytics, and automation to revolutionise the generation, distribution, and consumption of electrical power. From predictive maintenance to the seamless integration of renewable energy sources, Smart Grids showcase the power of AI to enhance efficiency, resilience, and sustainability in the energy sector.

Overview

Smart Grids represent a revolutionary advancement in the energy sector, leveraging Artificial Intelligence to transform traditional power grids into intelligent and dynamic systems. These grids utilise real-time data, analytics, and automation to enhance efficiency, reliability, and sustainability in the generation, distribution, and consumption of electrical power.

Key Components

1. Advanced Metering Infrastructure (AMI)
   AI-powered smart meters collect real-time data on energy consumption at individual locations. This data is used for precise billing, load forecasting, and identifying energy usage patterns.

2. Distributed Energy Resources (DERs)
   AI optimises the integration and management of DERs, such as solar panels, wind turbines, and energy storage systems. Algorithms balance the generation and consumption of energy in real-time.

3. Predictive Maintenance
   Machine learning algorithms analyse data from sensors and equipment to predict potential failures and schedule maintenance activities. This proactive approach minimises downtime and extends the lifespan of grid components.

4. Grid Optimisation
   AI optimises the operation of the grid by dynamically adjusting parameters such as voltage, frequency, and load distribution. This ensures efficient energy transfer and

minimises losses in transmission and distribution.

5. Demand Response
   AI enables demand response programmes by predicting peak demand periods and adjusting energy consumption accordingly. This helps utilities manage loads efficiently and avoid grid overloads during peak times.

Advantages of Smart Grids

1. Enhanced Grid Resilience
   Smart Grids are more resilient to disruptions and outages. AI algorithms detect faults and reroute power automatically, minimising the impact of failures.

2. Integration of Renewable Energy
   AI incorporates the efficient and seamless inclusion of renewable energy sources into the grid. It optimises the variability of renewable generation and ensures a stable power supply.

3. Improved Energy Efficiency
   By continuously monitoring and optimising grid operations, AI contributes to increased energy efficiency. This results in reduced energy losses during transmission and distribution.

4. Cost Savings
   Predictive maintenance and optimised grid operations lead to cost savings for utilities. Efficient load management and reduced downtime translate into financial benefits.

Challenges and Considerations

1. Cybersecurity
   As Smart Grids rely on interconnected digital systems, ensuring robust cybersecurity measures is crucial to protect

against potential cyber threats and unauthorised access.

2. Data Privacy
   Handling the vast amounts of data generated by Smart Grids requires careful consideration of data privacy regulations. Protecting consumer data and ensuring compliance with privacy laws is essential.

3. Interoperability
   Ensuring interoperability among various components and systems in Smart Grids is a challenge. Standardisation is necessary for seamless communication between different devices and technologies.

4. Public Perception and Acceptance
   Educating the public about the benefits and safety of Smart Grids is important. Addressing concerns related to privacy, health, and the environmental impact of new technologies is crucial for widespread acceptance.

Impact on the Energy Industry

Smart Grids have a profound impact on the energy industry

1. Grid Modernisation
   Smart Grids represent a significant step toward modernising ageing power infrastructure. They pave the way for a more adaptable and technologically advanced energy grid.

2. Integration of Renewable Energy
   AI-driven smart grids facilitate the integration of renewable energy sources, supporting the global transition towards a more sustainable and low-carbon energy mix.

3. Operational Efficiency
   The automation and optimisation capabilities of AI contribute to increased operational efficiency for utilities, reducing costs

and enhancing reliability.

4. Consumer Empowerment
   Smart Grids empower consumers by providing real-time information on energy consumption, enabling them to make informed decisions about usage and costs.
   Smart Grids exemplify how AI applications are transforming the energy sector, addressing challenges, and paving the way for a more sustainable and resilient energy future.

II. Algorithmic Trading in Finance

Embarking on a journey through the bustling realm of financial markets, this chapter explores the game-changing application of Artificial Intelligence in Algorithmic Trading. In the intricate world of finance, algorithms are not just lines of code; they are strategic architects of trades executed at speeds beyond human capability. Dive into the complexities of data analysis, risk management, and the elimination of emotional biases as we uncover how AI-driven algorithms have reshaped trading landscapes, reduced costs, and brought about a new era of efficiency in the financial industry.

Overview

Algorithmic Trading, also known as algo-trading or automated trading, involves the use of computer algorithms to implement trading strategies in financial markets. This application of AI has significantly transformed the landscape of financial trading by automating the decision-making process and executing trades at high speeds.

Key Components

1. Data Analysis and Pattern Recognition
   AI algorithms analyse vast amounts of financial data in real-

time, identifying patterns, trends, and potential trading opportunities. This includes market prices, trading volumes, news sentiment, and various economic indicators.

2. Algorithm Development
   Quantitative analysts and data scientists develop complex trading algorithms based on mathematical models, statistical analysis, and machine learning techniques. These algorithms aim to exploit market inefficiencies and generate profitable trades.

3. Execution Algorithms
   Execution algorithms are designed to optimise the timing and pricing of trades. They split large orders into smaller ones, execute trades across multiple venues, and manage the impact of trades on market prices.

4. Risk Management
   AI contributes substantially to addressing the risks inherent in algorithmic trading. It monitors market conditions, assesses potential risks, and adjusts trading parameters to avoid large losses.

Advantages of Algorithmic Trading

1. Speed and Efficiency
   Algorithms execute trades at speeds beyond human capability, responding to market changes in milliseconds. This efficiency is crucial in markets where prices can change rapidly.

2. Elimination of Emotional Bias
   AI-driven algorithms make decisions based on predefined rules and parameters, eliminating emotional biases that can influence human traders. This contributes to more objective and disciplined trading.

3. 24/7 Market Monitoring
   AI algorithms can continuously monitor global financial markets, identifying opportunities and executing trades 24/7. This is especially advantageous in markets with different time zones.

4. Backtesting and Optimisation
   Using historical data, algorithms can be backtested to assess their operational performance. This allows traders to optimise strategies, identify potential pitfalls, and refine algorithms before deploying them in real markets.

Challenges and Considerations

1. Algorithmic Complexity
   Developing sophisticated algorithms requires expertise in quantitative finance, machine learning, and programming. Ensuring the reliability and robustness of these algorithms is a continuous challenge.

2. Market Risks
   While algorithms are designed to minimise risks and enhance trading efficiency, unforeseen market events can sometimes lead to unexpected outcomes. One such event is a flash crash, where the prices of assets suddenly plummet within seconds or minutes, only to recover just as quickly. These abrupt drops can be triggered by a combination of factors, including high-frequency trading systems executing a large number of trades at lightning speed, technical glitches, or errors in trading orders. When multiple algorithms react to the same market signals simultaneously, it can create a cascade effect, rapidly driving down prices. Additionally, extreme volatility—sharp and unpredictable price swings—poses significant challenges. These rapid changes can strain algorithmic trading systems, potentially leading to substantial losses if not properly managed. Understanding and preparing

for such risks is crucial to maintaining stability and effectiveness in algorithmic trading.

3. Regulatory Compliance
   Algorithmic trading is subject to regulatory scrutiny. Compliance with regulations and ensuring that algorithms adhere to market rules and safeguards is essential.

4. Overreliance on Historical Data
   To predict future market movements, algorithms depend on historical data. Sudden market changes or unprecedented events may challenge the effectiveness of these predictions.

Impact on the Financial Industry

The rise of algorithmic trading has had a deep impact on the financial industry.

1. **Liquidity and Efficiency**
   Algorithmic trading contributes to market liquidity by facilitating efficient trade execution. It narrows bid-ask spreads and ensures that buyers and sellers can transact more easily.

2. **Reduced Trading Costs**
   The automation of trades and the elimination of manual processes reduce transaction costs. This benefits both institutional and retail investors.

3. **Market Accessibility**
   Algorithmic trading has democratised market access, allowing a broader range of market participants, including hedge funds, institutional investors, and retail traders, to engage in sophisticated trading strategies.

4. **Increased Competition**
   The rise of algorithmic trading has increased market competition. Traders must continually innovate and refine their algorithms to stay competitive in dynamic markets.

   Algorithmic trading exemplifies how AI applications in finance have evolved to enhance efficiency, reduce costs, and bring about transformative changes in traditional trading practices.

III. Personalised Learning Platforms in Education

Education is embracing a personalised revolution, and at the heart of this transformative shift lies Personalised Learning Platforms powered by Artificial Intelligence. Here we unravel the ways in which AI is reshaping traditional education models, tailoring learning experiences to the unique needs and preferences of each student. From adaptive learning algorithms to intelligent tutoring systems, we explore how AI fosters individualised skill development, improves engagement, and revolutionises the way we approach education.

Overview

Personalised Learning Platforms harness the power of Artificial Intelligence to tailor educational experiences to the unique needs, preferences, and learning styles of individual students. These platforms use advanced algorithms, data analytics, and adaptive technologies to create personalised learning journeys, revolutionising traditional education models.

Key Components

1. **Adaptive Learning Algorithms**
   AI-driven algorithms assess a student's performance, learning pace, and comprehension levels. Based on this data, the platform adapts the content and difficulty level to match the student's individual capabilities.

2. **Data Analytics and Learning Analytics**
   Continuous data analysis provides insights into student progress, strengths, and areas for improvement. Learning analytics inform educators and students about the effectiveness of different instructional strategies.

3. **Intelligent Tutoring Systems**
   Through real-time feedback and guidance, AI tutors assist students effectively. These systems adapt their teaching methods based on individual student responses, reinforcing concepts and addressing misconceptions.

4. **Personalised Content Delivery**
   AI platforms customise learning materials, including text, videos, and interactive exercises, to align with each student's learning preferences and goals. This ensures engagement and relevance in the learning process.

Advantages of Personalised Learning Platforms

1. **Tailored Learning Path**
   Personalised learning platforms offer individualised learning paths, allowing students to progress at their own pace and focus on areas that require more attention.

2. **Improved Engagement**
   By presenting content in diverse formats and adapting to individual learning styles, AI-powered platforms enhance student engagement and motivation.

3. **Targeted Intervention**
   AI identifies learning gaps and provides targeted interventions to address specific challenges, ensuring that students master foundational concepts before progressing.

4. **Data-Driven Decision-Making**
   Educators can make informed decisions based on real-time data, allowing for timely interventions, personalised support, and adjustments to instructional strategies.

Challenges and Considerations

1. **Data Privacy and Security**
   Protecting student data and ensuring privacy is a paramount concern. AI platforms must comply with stringent data protection regulations to maintain trust.

2. **Equity and Access**
   Ensuring equal access to personalised learning platforms for all students, regardless of socio-economic factors, is a challenge that requires addressing issues related to digital infrastructure and resources.

3. **Teacher Training and Support**
   For the effective use of AI tools, educators need training in integrating them into their teaching practices. Continuous support is essential to ensure that teachers can leverage the full potential of personalised learning platforms.

4. **Ethical Considerations**
   Ethical concerns, such as algorithmic bias and the potential for reinforcing stereotypes, must be carefully addressed to ensure fair and unbiased learning experiences.

Impact on Education

Personalised Learning Platforms have a profound impact on the education landscape

1. **Individualised Skill Development**
   Students can focus on developing specific skills and competencies based on their unique strengths and interests.

2. **Lifelong Learning**
   Personalised learning encourages a lifelong learning mindset, as individuals can pursue education at their own pace and throughout various stages of life.

3. **Inclusive Learning**
   AI helps address diverse learning needs, making education more inclusive for students with different abilities and learning styles.

4. **Data-Informed Teaching**
   Educators benefit from actionable insights, enabling them to make data-informed decisions and provide targeted support to each student.

   Personalised Learning Platforms represent a transformative approach to education, harnessing the capabilities of AI to create more adaptive, engaging, and effective learning experiences for students of all ages.

GLOSSARY

1. **Algorithm**
   A step-by-step process or set of rules followed by a computer to solve a problem.
   Example: AI uses algorithms to recognise patterns in data.

2. **Artificial Intelligence (AI)**
   Machines or software that can think, learn, and make decisions like humans.
   Example: Siri and Alexa use AI to understand voice commands.

3. **Artificial General Intelligence (AGI)**
   A theoretical AI system that can perform any intellectual task that a human can do.
   Example: A robot that thinks, learns, and acts like a human in every way.

4. **Artificial Narrow Intelligence (ANI)**
   AI that is designed for a specific task rather than general reasoning.
   Example: AI that plays chess but cannot drive a car.

5. **Artificial Superintelligence (ASI)**
   A future AI that surpasses human intelligence in every aspect.
   Example: A self-improving AI that can solve all human problems.

6. **Automation**
   Using AI to complete tasks without human intervention.
   Example: Self-checkout machines at supermarkets use automation.

7. **Big Data**
   Extremely large sets of data that AI uses to learn and make decisions.
   Example: Social media platforms analyse big data to show relevant ads.

8. **Bias in AI**
   When AI systems produce unfair or prejudiced outcomes due to flawed training data.
   Example: AI rejecting loan applications from certain groups unfairly.

9. **Chatbot**
   AI software that interacts with humans through text or voice.
   Example: Customer support bots on websites.

10. **Computer Vision**
    AI's capability to interpret and process visual content, including images and videos.
    Example: Face recognition on smartphones uses computer vision.

11. **Data Mining**
    The process of finding useful patterns in large datasets.
    Example: Online stores use data mining to recommend products.

12. **Data Science**
    The study of analysing and interpreting large amounts of data.
    Example: AI experts use data science to train machine learning models.

13. **Deep Learning**
    A subset of AI that mimics how human brains process information using neural networks.
    Example: AI recognising handwriting is powered by deep learning.

14. **Ethics in AI**
    The moral concerns around AI decision-making and its impact on society.
    Example: Should AI be allowed to decide who gets a job interview?

15. **Expert System**
    AI designed to mimic human experts in a specific field.
    Example: AI doctors diagnosing diseases.

16. **Facial Recognition**
    AI technology that identifies people from images or videos.
    Example: Airports use facial recognition for security checks.

17. **Feature Engineering**
    Selecting and modifying data to improve AI learning.
    Example: Choosing the best customer behaviour data for AI-driven marketing.

18. **Federated Learning**
    A way to train AI without sharing private data.
    Example: Smartphones improving autocorrect without sending data to a central server.

19. **Generative AI**
    AI that creates new content like images, music, or text.
    Example: AI-generated artwork and deepfake videos.

20. **GPT (Generative Pre-trained Transformer)**
    An AI model that generates human-like text.
    Example: AI chatbots like ChatGPT use GPT technology.

21. **Hyperparameter Tuning**
    Adjusting AI settings to improve its performance.
    Example: Finding the best learning speed for a self-driving car AI.

22. **Image Recognition**
    AI's ability to identify objects in pictures.
    Example: AI detecting cats and dogs in photos.

23. **Inference**
    The process of AI making decisions based on what it has learned.
    Example: AI predicting tomorrow's weather based on past data.
24. **Internet of Things (IoT)**
    Internet-enabled devices that gather, exchange, and transmit data.
    Example: AI-powered smart thermostats adjusting home temperature.

25. **Language Model**
    AI trained to understand and generate human language.
    Example: Google Translate uses language models.

26. **Machine Learning (ML)**
    AI that improves over time by learning from data.
    Example: Netflix's recommendation system learns from what you watch.

27. **Model Training**
    Teaching an AI system using data to improve its performance.
    Example: AI learning to recognise spam emails.

28. **Neural Network**
    An AI structure inspired by the human brain, used in deep learning.
    Example: AI-powered speech recognition uses neural

networks.

29. **Natural Language Processing (NLP)**
    AI's ability to understand and interpret human language.
    Example: AI assistants like Alexa use NLP to process voice commands.

30. **Overfitting**
    When AI learns too much from training data and performs poorly on new data.
    Example: An AI that memorises past stock prices but can't predict future trends.

31. **Pattern Recognition**
    AI detecting recurring trends in data.
    Example: AI spotting fraudulent credit card transactions.

32. **Personalised AI**
    AI that adapts to individual preferences.
    Example: Spotify suggesting songs based on your listening history.

33. **Predictive Analytics**
    AI predicting future outcomes based on past data.
    Example: AI forecasting sales for an online store.

34. **Quantum AI**
    AI powered by quantum computing for complex problem-solving.
    Example: AI using quantum mechanics for medical research.

35. **Reinforcement Learning**
    AI learning by trial and error to maximise rewards.
    Example: AI teaching itself to play video games.

36. **Recurrent Neural Network (RNN)**
    An AI model designed to handle sequential data, recognising patterns over time.

Example: AI predicting the next word in a sentence.

37. **Robotic Process Automation (RPA)**
    AI performing repetitive business tasks without human effort.
    Example: AI handling invoice processing in banks.

38. **Self-Supervised Learning**
    AI training itself without human-labelled data.
    Example: AI understanding videos without pre-written descriptions.

39. **Sentiment Analysis**
    AI determining emotions in text.
    Example: AI analysing social media posts to detect public opinion.

40. **Speech Recognition**
    AI understanding and processing spoken words.
    Example: AI voice assistants like Google Assistant use speech recognition.

41. **Supervised Learning**
    AI learning with labelled examples.
    Example: AI trained with pictures labelled as 'cat' or 'dog' to recognise animals.

42. **Swarm Intelligence**
    AI mimicking group behaviour seen in nature, like ant colonies.
    Example: AI coordinating drones in a swarm for search missions.

43. **Synthetic Data**
    Artificially generated data used for training AI.
    Example: AI learning from simulated customer transactions.

44. **Turing Test**
    A test to check if AI can think like a human.

Example: AI passing the Turing Test if humans can't tell it's a machine.

45. **Transfer Learning**
    AI using knowledge from one task to improve another.
    Example: AI trained on English texts helping with French translations.

46. **Unsupervised Learning**
    AI learning patterns in data without labels.
    Example: AI grouping customers based on their shopping habits.

47. **Virtual Assistant**
    AI that helps users with tasks through voice or text commands.
    Example: Apple's Siri is a virtual assistant.

48. **Weak AI**
    AI designed for a limited task, without true understanding.
    Example: A chess-playing AI that doesn't understand emotions.

49. **XAI (Explainable AI)**
    AI designed to help users understand the logic behind AI-driven decisions.
    Example: AI justifying why it rejected a loan application.

50. **Zero-Shot Learning**
    AI understanding new tasks without prior training.
    Example: AI recognising a new animal it has never seen before.

About the Authors

Mr. Kalyanjit Hatibaruah is the **Chairman of Flugelsoft Group**, leading a portfolio of companies specialising in various tech and management domains. Holding a BTech degree in Electronics & Communication from NIT Kurukshetra, Haryana, and an MBA from Pune University, he possesses a robust academic foundation complemented by extensive experience in technology stacks, including Ecommerce, Distributed Applications, AI/ML, and Web3. Recognised as a pioneer in Blockchain Applications, he serves as an adviser and leads tech teams on financial projects involving Blockchain and Tokenisation.

An accomplished technology management professional with diverse experience in technology and consulting across multidisciplinary domains, Mr. Hatibaruah is also a renowned public speaker. He frequently addresses topics such as **Web3, Metaverse, Artificial Intelligence, Entrepreneurship, Start-up Ecosystems, and Angel Investing** at business schools, universities, and corporate events.

A committed mentor and investor, Mr. Hatibaruah is an **Angel Investor** with Mumbai Angels and collaborates with numerous start-up incubators and accelerators as a mentor. He is actively involved in incubation programmes at STPI (Gurgaon & Pune), T-Hub, India Accelerator, Jagriti Enterprise Centre Purvanchal (Deoria), and

European incubators, particularly focusing on Web3, AI, Metaverse, Blockchain, and emerging technologies. He also invests in start-ups, guiding them in incubation and go-to-market strategies.

His contributions to education and innovation include conducting workshops and offering courses—both online and offline—across diverse topics, including university-level programmes. He was a **Judge at the Smart India Hackathon** 2022-2023 for the Hardware and Software Edition under the Ministry of Education, Government of India. Additionally, he frequently serves as a Judge for national and international hackathons, including the India International Science Festival, and is invited to prestigious events hosted by universities such as IITs, IIMs, and AIIMS.

As a podcast host, Mr. Hatibaruah runs "**Web3 Unleashed**" in partnership with Pod One Entertainment, available on major podcast platforms. His thought leadership extends to mentoring professionals, students, and start-ups to successfully enter and thrive in various industries, offering invaluable guidance on leveraging emerging technologies.

A visionary with a global network, Mr. Hatibaruah maintains strong connections with venture capitalists and professionals across diverse fields. His extensive knowledge and industry experience make him a sought-after resource for those seeking to explore or excel in technology, management, and innovation.

Connect with Kalyanjit Hatibaruah on social media:

Linkedin:
https://www.linkedin.com/in/kalyanjit

Facebook:
https://www.facebook.com/kalyanjit

About the Authors

Pratibha Das Hatibaruah is a seasoned technology **entrepreneur and founder of Flugelsoft**, a leading Web3 company specialising in Blockchain, Metaverse, and AI. With 24+ years of experience, she has led innovative product development teams and advised start-ups, earning recognition as an influencer in the Web3 space.

Her extensive experience in technical writing has honed her ability to break down complex technological concepts into accessible, user-friendly content. As a Content Specialist, she has spearheaded diverse projects, leading teams of technical writers, designers, and digital marketers to produce high-quality documentation across multiple verticals, including user manuals, white papers, API documentation, and more.

Certified as a **Microsoft Certified System Engineer (MCSE)** and **Cisco Certified Network Associate (CCNA)**, Pratibha began her career as a Network Engineer at top MNCs like Toyota Kirloskar Motors and Infosys, Bengaluru, before transitioning into entrepreneurship.

Pratibha hosts her **podcast channel,** PRATIBHA'S TECHTALK, where she delves into Web3 technologies and their impact on industries. She has also created educational content for the Web3 space on **Udemy** and produces videos for her **YouTube channel**, PRATIBHA'S TECHTALK ON METAVERSE.

Her dynamic presence extends to international conferences and universities as an **industry speaker.** She has delivered talks at esteemed venues, including IIT Guwahati, Tura University, J.C. Bose University of Science & Technology, YMCA Faridabad, Assam Engineering Institute (AEI), Marathwada Mitra Mandal's College of Engineering Pune, and Srimad Andavan Arts and Science College, Trichy, among many others.

Pratibha is also a **business mentor**, guiding start-ups and entrepreneurs in the northeast region of India through programmes such as Jagriti Enterprise Centre Purvanchal (JECP) and Tejaswini (an initiative of the Women's Cell, Industries & Commerce Department, Government of Assam, in collaboration with NEHHDC), alongside several other regional and national initiatives aimed at fostering entrepreneurship and innovation.

As an avid **tech blogger**, Pratibha shares insights on her blog, PRATIBHA'S TECH TALK and contributes to global platforms such as *Medium*, *Momspresso*, THUMBPRINT, TWIST AND TWAIN, and BLASTING NEWS. She has also written for national publications like THE ASSAM TRIBUNE and ARUNACHAL24, covering technology, digital marketing, lifestyle, and industry writing.

Though her career is largely defined by technology and entrepreneurship, Pratibha leads a "double life" as a novelist. Under the pen name PRATIBHA R DH, she has authored seven fiction books, including CHILD OF PARADISE (LISTEN TO YOUR DREAMS), a paranormal crime mystery, and BUTTERFLIES IN THE STORM, a romantic suspense novel—both **Amazon bestsellers**. Balancing these contrasting domains is challenging, but her passion for both keeps her journey dynamic and fulfilling.

Connect with Pratibha Das Hatibaruah on social media:

Linkedin:
https://www.linkedin.com/in/web3pratibha

Facebook:
https://www.facebook.com/BlockchainEntrepreneurr

Instagram (Tech Channel):
https://www.instagram.com/pratibha_blockchain_techie

Instagram (Fiction Author):
https://www.instagram.com/author.pratibha

Blog:
https://pratibhastechtalk.wordpress.com

www.ingramcontent.com/pod-product-compliance
Ingram Content Group UK Ltd.
Pitfield, Milton Keynes, MK11 3LW, UK
UKHW021406190726
13845UKWH00028B/913

9 789334 219777